DAWN
AFTER
DACHAU

DAWN
AFTER
DACHAU

by

JOEL SACK

SHENGOLD PUBLISHERS, INC.
NEW YORK

ISBN 0-88400-141-5
Library of Congress Catalog Card Number: 90-53264
Copyright © 1990 by Joel Sack

Published by Shengold Publishers, Inc.
18 W. 45th St., New York, N.Y. 10036

Printed in the United States of America

*To Gina, my wife
and my inspiration.*

*My profound gratitude to my friends, Ed and Lois Grayson,
for their help in publishing this work.*

EXEGI MONUMENTUM AERE PERENNIUS REGALIQUE
SITU PIRAMIDUM ALTIUS, QUOD NON IMBER EDAX,
NON AQUILO IMPOTENS DOSSIT DIRUERE. . . . .

HORACE

CARMINUM LIBER III. ODE XXX

I have completed a memorial more
lasting than bronze and higher
than the royal grave of the pyramids,
that neither biting rain nor the north
wind in its fury can destroy. . . . .

INTRODUCTION

Millions of pages have been written about the Holocaust. Obviously, none of the writing will convey the horror of the unimaginable crimes the Germans committed to achieve their goal: no more and no less than mass-murdering all the Jewish people.

Some time after the American army had liberated the Dachau Concentration Camp it occurred to me that it is also important to record events which followed the liberation, the struggles for freedom which the liberated prisoners, particularly the Jews, had to endure after that momentous event. They were liberated from the concentration camp in Dachau on that memorable April 29, 1945. But by no means were they yet free people.

For many weeks, we still remained imprisoned within the walls and barbed wire fences of the former concentration camp. American G.I.'s took over guarding the main gate. Inmates were not allowed out of the camp.

For weeks, liberated men continued to die in great numbers from typhus, exhaustion, and because their emaciated bodies could no longer digest food. Tragically, no hospitals were made available in the nearby city of Munich or in the town of Dachau. The sick and the dying were placed in hastily organized *lazarets*, primitive hospitals, within the compound. Most of the sick died. Probably with proper medical care, many more would have lived.

A cemetery was established for those who died after the liberation. Former prisoners of all nationalities and religions were buried side by side. Crosses and Stars of David intermingled in the straight rows.

Some highly positioned occupational officials showed outright resentment toward the liberated inmates. They perceived us as a nuisance, an obstacle to smooth administration over the newly submissive German population.

Most of the liberated were moved to specially organized camps, still living under very primitive conditions. We were also given a new name, D.P.'s, for Displaced Persons. The camps in which we lived began to be called D.P. camps.

Some medical care was at first provided for the sick survivors. Amazingly, no thought whatsoever was given to the mental and psychological needs of the victims.

In a few extreme cases of exhaustion, survivors were taken to sanatoriums. In general, the liberated were left to their own wits to fend for their daily existence on the meager rations of the D.P. camps.

Survivors of most nationalities liberated in Dachau were not subjected to these deprivations for any significant length of time. They were repatriated within weeks and usually were given celebrations when they arrived home. Only some Poles and Russians, who for their own good reasons, refused to be repatriated, remained in Germany.

For the Jews, it was different. Jewish survivors had no choice but to remain in the American Zone of West Germany, mostly in D.P. camps. Some who went back to their countries of origin, met such hatred and even organized pogroms, as in Poland, that they were forced to flee their countries.

Most Jewish D.P.'s renounced their citizenships in East European countries, and claimed the status of stateless persons. They did this hoping and expecting that eventually a solution to the situation of the homeless would be found.

Many younger and some older individuals were determined to go to Palestine, disregarding the dangers of what the English called the "illegal *aliyah*" immigration. England, on land and high seas, fought against the miserable survivors of the German death camps. They ruthlessly interned Palestine-bound Jews in detention camps which they established on the Greek island of Cyprus. Other Jews were cruelly returned by force to Germany.

When the United States Congress finally passed special legislation to accept a limited number of survivors, long lines formed in front of U.S. consulates.

Difficult conditions had to be met in order to qualify. Applicants had to secure affidavits from citizens or organizations in the United States. The affidavits had to guarantee that the applicants would never become a public burden or require welfare support after entering the States. The requirement that only healthy applicants could immigrate to the United States caused fear and anxiety.

Applicants were subjected to very rigorous medical screenings for physical and mental fitness. Then came the anxious wait for results. There were pitiful cases of despair when a rejected individual felt guilt for causing misfortune to his family, who would not leave behind a recovering family member.

It was a long and troublesome road to freedom after the liberation of Dachau. There were many good and understanding friends who helped in the recovery. But other people found it too difficult to realize that the survivors were decent, innocent people who just happened to be caught up in the most barbaric mass capture and murder in European history. Often doctors who were sent to heal the liberated, treated their medical colleagues among the survivors with rude slights as if the survivors were individuals of lower standing. This was degrading and painful for people who had barely escaped death.

As time passed, the occupational forces started to use

German militia for auxiliary police functions. This was deeply resented by the survivors.

In March 1946, the German militia surrounded the Stuttgart Jewish D.P. camp and staged an unprovoked raid on the Jews, pretending to search for arms. The inmates became enraged. Although unarmed, all, including women, furiously charged the militiamen. The Germans fired and a number of Jewish inmates were injured. One was killed. The American military police finally arrived and ordered the Germans out of the camp.

News of that ugly incident, a reminder of the too-well-remembered German actions in Jewish ghettos, reverberated through the D.P. camps, and all over the world. It caused bitter resentment toward those in the occupational administration who were responsible for the raid.

More suffering was caused by painful, usually accidental information about communities, families, and individuals who had perished. Rare reunions of relatives, friends, and sometime spouses were the joyous occasions.

Orphaned men and women sought solace in each others' company. Sometimes it was the beginning of a romantic union rebuilding two lives. In a few cases, this was sadly disturbed by the surprise appearance of a spouse who had been reported dead. Either the old marriage might be saved, or a divorce could be agreed on by the newly married. Although painful, these events were usually accomplished with remarkable charity and understanding.

To satisfy their need for the old traditions of the Jewish people, the survivors often turned to observance of the religious Commandments. This was surprising considering the bitter doubts the persecuted so often had expressed about a Divine Presence.

The Zionist idea of rebuilding a Jewish country in the ancient land of Biblical Israel was universally shared by the survivors. It was their ardent expression of hope for a safer and better future in a Jewish State.

The road from Dachau to freedom after the liberation was long and painful. It was a road full of surprises, a mixture of sorrows and joys on the way to a new beginning.

ONE

Konzentrationslager
Concentration Camp, Dachau

In Barrack No. 19 the line of prisoners formed for evening chow. For days no bread had been issued. Everybody was anxious to receive the gruel, a dark liquid in which floated rare pieces of potato or turnip. This would be the one meal of the day. Each man held some kind of bowl, pot or tin can. The gruel hopefully would ease the ceaseless hunger pains.

The afternoon sun was still bright and warm. The coming of spring was in the air. I had always loved this special season when life was triumphing over the death of the winter past.

Was spring predicting my own survival? The rays of the sun soothed my body. Sitting on the rough plank floor, I adjusted my back and head to receive the full sun.

The barrack was unusually quiet. The food line advanced very slowly. My bony buttocks ached.

My feet would support me for only a short while. I was exhausted and emaciated after the recent death march from the concentration camp Flossenburg. It had lasted six days and nights. Only a few hundred prisoners, exhausted to their limits, survived the march to Dachau. Those of the 6,000 or so prisoners who could not keep up were mercilessly gunned down by the uniformed Germans, who formed a tight guard on both sides of the human column.

It was night when we arrived at the Dachau gates. They were closed. The guards ordered us to sit on the wet snow. We huddled together as tightly as we could to keep warm, while huge flakes of an April snow shower were covering us with a frozen blanket.

Over the gate to the camp a sign proclaimed:

ARBEIT MACHT FREI, Work Makes Us Free.

The next morning the gates opened and those who had survived the night on the snowy ground were marched into the camp. The admission process had lasted several hours. Finally we were admitted to Barrack No. 19.

All of a sudden, the food line moved, and I was jolted back to the present. I was about half way to the gruel kettle when suddenly the barrack door flew open with a crash. A prisoner rushed in and screamed, *"Die Americaner sind hier. Die sind im Lager.* The Americans are here. They are in the camp."

At first the message was lost on me. In the immediate melee, I was worried, I wouldn't get my portion of the gruel. My next thought was, "Am I already a muselman, a goner?" How was it possible that I could worry about not getting my bowl of lousy gruel? How could that be? How, I thought, could these Americans arrive so late, at the last moment, for me to survive? My mind was as exhausted as my body.

I pushed myself against the wall so I would not be trampled by the wildly milling crowd. The able-bodied men began to dance and sing. Most of them were crying. Others, who could not comprehend freedom, showed no reaction.

Why did freedom come so unexpectedly? Was it real or was hope just a narcotic that took us out of our hellish reality?

It seemed that freedom was here, but the hour was, for countless many, too late. I, for one, was practically a vegetable, ready to wither away in a very short time. Perhaps there was a spark of hope.

On this note of optimism, I struggled against exhaustion, apathy, and hunger cramps, to drag myself outdoors. What was going on?

In the distance, I saw a mob of prisoners at the main gate, and along the inner wire fence. A skeleton-like tall fellow, who could see over other people's heads, was reporting excitedly in Polish, "The Americans are rounding up the guards. They are pulling down the guards who are still up on towers. They're lining them up against the fence. It looks like they're going to shoot them."

We heard a burst of machine-gun fire, and our announcer happily yelled out, "They shot them. They killed all the sons of German whores!"

Most of the crowd was jubilant. Somehow, I remained apathetic and unable to share the happiness. My tiredness was like lead. It overtook my body and mind. I dragged myself back to the barrack, found my bunk, and lay down. I closed my hurting eyes, and lost myself in oblivion.

When I opened my eyes again, I shared the bunk with only two other fellows. Until now we had been sleeping five or six to a bunk. Like sardines in a can, we could manage it only by pointing our feet and heads alternately in opposite directions. Even at this, we had to lie on our sides, and could not change positions for the rest of the night.

Some fellows would die in their sleep. The living kept sharing the bunk with the corpses until the morning roll call whistle. Then assigned inmates carried out the corpses and laid them in front of the barrack to be counted meticulously during the morning roll call. The corpses were then dragged to the crematorium.

Next to me, the two fellows were sleeping, oblivious to the world. The eyeballs deep in their sockets, the sharply protruding cheek bones, and the skeletal bodies showed their far gone emaciation. With special medical attention, they might have a slim chance to survive. At the moment, they were unaware that they had just been liberated.

I came out of my stupor when I heard a commotion in the barrack. Some inmates were moving among the bunks, distributing a big loaf of bread and a large can of beef conserve to each man.

I attacked the food and devoured it. The air became filled with festivity. Half of the bread and most of the meat were gone in an incredibly short time. It came to me that I could get sick from devouring so much rich food when I had been starving. I forced myself to put the rest of the bread and meat aside. There ensued a battle with myself which I kept losing. I had no will power to resist the food. At short intervals, I was reaching for it, and then pushing it away again. So bit by bit, I consumed everything. My pauses were short, but they may have been good for me. Around me, men became very sick shortly after the meal. I felt the pains of a very full stomach, but it was a welcome feeling I had not experienced in a very long time.

A few hours later, a heavenly aroma filled the barrack. A kettle with soup for the evening meal was carried in. Soup it was this time, full of pork with a thick layer of golden fat on the surface. It was hardly a liquid. The sight and the smell made us ecstatic.

Each man got a full bowl of this wonderful stuff, and then there were second and third helpings. A feast of delicious food ensued.

The disaster caused by that feast came later. Moaning from diarrhea and severe abdominal cramps never ceased the whole night. Many did not survive. The rich, plentiful food, provided out of the goodness of the hearts of our liberators, was a mistake. They did not know any better. The soldiers with kind hearts just did not have any experience in handling exhaustion, starvation, and every other possible kind of suffering. Many men died of feasting.

The morning rows of corpses in front of the barracks increased for days to come. The improvised hospital in the camp overflowed with cases of typhus, dysentery, and emaciation. Big, fat lice continued to feast on our bodies.

I suffered an aggravated diarrhea. Because of my aversion to pork, ingrained from childhood in the kosher household of my parents, I consumed only little of the meat. What probably saved my life was that after the soup feast, I had dropped off into a restless sleep, oblivious of the suffering and misery around me.

But my sleep was a nightmare. In my dream I was again in the death march from Concentration Camp Flossenburg. With painful clarity, I relived the effort of the condemned marchers to go on, to keep moving or be shot by one of the German guards. In my dream, the fellow next to me started to fall back from his line. The next dream picture was of a middle-aged German guard aiming his rifle at the head of the victim, who desperately tried to regain his place in line. A shot rang out. The skull of the struggling marcher exploded. Bits of brain sprayed around, covering other marchers with a bloody pulp.

The shot of the guard's rifle was so real that I woke up with a start, soaked in perspiration, wondering if I were awake or still dreaming, because gun shots rang out in the air. Suddenly I realized that I was hearing real gunfire, machine-gun salvos not far from the camp.

I was wide awake with fear. My mind raced over the events which had taken place only hours ago. I sat up on my bunk, and tried to recall every detail of what had happened. Was liberation another fiction of my feverish mind? No, on the side of my bunk I could see the empty can of meat conserve. The reality started to come into focus.

Yes, it must be true. The Americans had entered the camp a few hours ago. Inmates were shouting, dancing, and singing. The Americans had rounded up and shot the guards. It had really happened. But why the machine-gun fire now?

The fire seemed to intensify. I was struck by fear that what happened a number of weeks ago in Concentration Camp Flossenburg might now be repeated here in Dachau.

I clearly recalled Flossenburg. For days, heavy guns had reverberated in the distance. Prisoners with military experience excitedly said that the front could not be far away. Especially at night, the roar of guns shook us and awoke hope of liberation in us 30,000 inmates.

Then one morning, white flags appeared on the watchtowers around the camp. They looked to me like white-winged angels of deliverance. The camp's SS units fled into the woods of the Czech Mountains, leaving only a few guards on the watchtowers.

I joined the throng of prisoners on the roll call square for a noisy celebration. Even some of the guards on the towers tossed packs of cigarettes into the crowd of prisoners. I was so proud of myself when I jumped up and snatched one of the packs out of the air. A Russian inmate exclaimed, *"Eta molodec.* What a guy!" His admiration is still with me. I smoked most of the cigarettes and got delightfully dizzy from the heavy dose of unaccustomed nicotine.

Suddenly, the sound of the distant guns was no more, and the white flags disappeared from the watchtowers. The SS troops returned to the camp, and renewed their rule of terror and death. The rumors were that for unknown reasons, the American army had turned north and bypassed the Flossenburg Concentration Camp. Just after midnight, loud shouts resounded in all barracks. *"Alle Juden H'raus.* All Jews out." The guards announced that anyone who disobeyed would be shot on the spot.

I decided that I was not going to cooperate. I tore the yellow Star of David patch off the left breast of my jacket, above the white and red patch which designated my Polish nationality. I stayed on my bunk trembling with fear as screaming Jewish inmates were dragged outdoors.

After the morning roll call, I didn't dare get in the gruel line. I was afraid of being recognized by some Jew-hating prisoner. Following the afternoon roll call, under the cover of darkness, I walked over to the barrack to locate three of my close friends dating back to the Plaszow Concentration Camp. The two Luxemburgers, Carl Thiel and Carl Brown, and the Czech, Dr. Strunz, were all very happy that I had escaped the trucks that were hauling Jews away.

They gave me a piece of bread and asked me to stay in touch. It was close to curfew. I started back, breaking off pieces of the bread in my pocket, and eating hungrily. A silhouette of an inmate passed and whispered in Yiddish, "A piece of bread, please, please." The man could not have known that I was secretly eating bread. He was probably just desperately hungry. At first I passed the man, but a sudden compassion took hold of me. I turned back, caught up with the man, and gave him a piece of my bread. Nothing said, each a stranger in this common tragedy, we parted into the darkness of the Concentration Camp Flossenburg.

Next morning the loudspeakers announced that all inmates of the camp would be divided into five columns of about 6,000 men each, and the camp would be evacuated that very day. Thus started six days of hell, the death march.

One day of the march, I heard the despairing voices of two sons imploring their father to go on, to make another effort and not to give up. They supported him on both sides and were dragging him along, hoping to save him from being shot by a guard. The old man begged them to abandon him, to go on and save their own lives. A shot rang out. The two sons were forced to move on under the blows of the German guards who had just killed their father.

Intensified machine-gun fire around the camp brought me out of the nightmare into the reality of Dachau. A terror took hold of me. Was it possible that the unforgettable nightmare of Flossenburg was going to repeat itself? Would the Germans regain control of the camp from the Americans? I shook with fear.

Hours later the sound of battle died away. It was early morning. The block elder explained to the nervous inmates that the American liberators had intercepted German troops approaching the camp from the direction of Munich. The Germans' goal was to recapture the camp with its 33,000 inmates, and carry out Himmler's order to annihilate every single prisoner. The order to all German military units had demanded that no prisoner was to get into the hands of the Americans alive. The elder assured us that although there had been American casualties, the Germans were repulsed, and the camp was safe again.

Dozing off, I was startled by the morning whistle. The thought of another roll call for the living and the still warm corpses was dreadful. I didn't think I had the strength for it. Amazingly, no order was given to file out of the barrack. The men milled around, strangely relaxed. The Americans must still be in control. I tried to put recent events together.

The Americans had entered the camp on the previous day, late in the afternoon. It was April 1945. But what day of the week? I didn't know.

Just recently I had turned 30. I was worn out, a skeleton in a loosely hanging, wrinkled skin. I could hardly walk. In fact, I had difficulty staying in a sitting position for any length of time. My feet were sore. My legs were weak and worn out. A thought came to me. How lucky I was to have had those wonderful leather shoes on my feet during the march. With the wooden clogs many men had, I surely would not have lasted very long. I smiled at the badly worn-out shoes on my feet.

When I had arrived at the Flossenburg Concentration Camp, I was restricted to a quarantine barrack of the prisoners with whom I had been transported in tightly packed cattle cars from Concentration Camp Plaszow. During the second miserable week of the quarantine, a Russian boy got close to the steel fence and we struck up a conversation. My Star of David made him curious. He wanted to know its meaning and origin.

During the next few days the boy used every opportunity to seek my companionship and ask questions about the Jews. Once, during a conversation about German atrocities in Poland and Russia, I caught a special expression on his face. I was touched by the tearful sadness in his blue eyes, which seemed far away. I moved closer to the fence and whispered, "Misha, aren't you Jewish?" The boy paled and heatedly protested that he was Russian and Christian. Agitated, he turned away from the fence and left.

I did not see Misha for a few days. Then he appeared one afternoon, short of breath and obviously scared. It had been announced in his barrack that he was assigned to a transport that would leave the next morning for an unknown destination. Since he was going to have to leave all his belongings behind, it occurred to Misha that he should give his good leather shoes to me, his newly acquired friend in the quarantine barrack. Misha kept talking as he took off his treasured shoes and exchanged them for my wooden clogs. All the time, he seemed to be holding something back. Suddenly he whispered, "I am a Jew. So far I have been able to hide it. But who knows how much longer? I'll always remember you."

With tears in his eyes, Misha left without looking back.

Now, here I was, looking at the badly worn shoes which had saved my life, and wondering what had happened after they took him away.

Breakfast on the first morning after liberation was an unbelievable feast. Scrambled eggs, bread, and coffee. As many helpings as we wanted. What a difference! No more shouting, no more beating, kicking, cursing. A different kind of order had arrived and humane conditions came with it. The rules of civilization were taking hold again.

I cleaned my utensils under a faucet in the washroom and went back to my bunk. Now that I had eaten, sleep was what I needed most. The bunk was empty. The two fellows who had shared the bunk with me did not make it. Their corpses had just been removed. I slept.

When I woke up, I remembered that on admission to the barrack, I had changed my name by adding "ski" at the end to show that I was a Polish Christian. A powerful urge came over me to correct this.

I dragged myself to the cubicle of the block elder, a Polish priest known as Anton. He was a tall, skinny man of indeterminate age, bald with only a remnant of gray hair looping a ring around his shiny skull. His black eyes had a quality of compassion.

Anton invited me to enter. I was very nervous and did not know how to start. Anton helped with a smile and asked if there was a problem.

I told him that at the registration, I had given my name

as Yulian Sakowski, Polish Catholic. My real name was Yoel
Sack and I was Jewish. Would Anton please make this cor-
rection in the block registration book right now, in my
presence? It was very important to me.

Anton took the registration book from a cabinet. After
turning some pages, he stopped, took a pen, and crossed out,
"Yulian Sakowski, Polish, Catholic, Engineer" and wrote instead, "Yoel Sack, Polish, Jewish, Engineer."

This done Anton got up and without saying a word, shook
my hand. Happy that my request had been satisfied, I went
back to my bunk. Physically and emotionally drained, I
nevertheless felt relieved and unburdened. I was overcome
by a very good feeling about myself. It was like returning
from an almost endless journey. It was as if I had just been
reborn. Now I was myself again with all my past, and all the
tradition that belonged to my person. My name was again
Yoel Sack.

Now, even if I did not survive Dachau after the liberation,
my true name would be on the long list of victims of this infamous place. I was again Yoel, the son of Israel and Frieda,
the grandson of Baruch and Debora and Shlomo and Rebec-
ca, the great grandson of Yoel, a descendant of the ancient
tribe of Levi. I was myself again.

TWO

Regaining my identity made me feel so good that I decided to go out and explore the liberated camp. The change was unbelievable. Inmates were milling around, joining in animated conversations. Even laughter filled the air in some places. I walked toward the main gate. Here and there, American officers and soldiers were surrounded by inmates. Their lively conversations were aided by vigorous gesticulations needed because of the different languages.

Coming out from between the two rows of barracks, I could see to the right the main gate. I walked slowly across the roll call square. The Jourhous gate, as it was called, was closed and guarded by American soldiers. Inmates were gathered there, but no one was allowed through the gate.

An American officer came toward me. "Hello," he said, with an engaging smile. Out of his pocket he pulled a small round tin and offered it to me. I stopped and examined the gift. It was instant coffee. I was exhausted and returned to my barrack.

Some survivors of the Flossenburg death march were sitting out front. I showed them the American coffee, and suggested that we taste it. Somebody lit a fire, burning pages of a German magazine he had been reading. When the water came to a boil, I opened the can and spilled its contents into the pot.

An incredible thing happened. The rich, strong aroma of real coffee filled the air. The smell was indescribably wonderful. In an instant, it brought back memories from a life almost as distant as another world.

We sat around the fire in silent concentration. A kind of

21

magic took over. Nobody moved and nobody said anything for a while. Then the men started to spoon the coffee out of the bowl, making sure everybody had his turn. The taste was as good as the aroma.

Yurek came over and sat down next to me. He was one of the five who at the start of the march from Flossenburg had made a pact to stick together. Realizing that this was going to be a deadly journey we had exchanged personal information about each other. Whoever survived would notify the kin of those who did not. The other four knew that I was Jewish, but I was confident that they would not betray me. When somebody suggested that one of us be designated leader of our small group, they unanimously agreed on me.

Mietek, 19, was the youngest of us. A university student, at the start of the war, he was physically fragile and sensitive. He seemed to be in a world of dreams. The shock of being kidnapped by Germans on the street like a homeless dog was still with him. We affectionately called him the virgin.

Olek was about to graduate as an architect at the start of the war when he was drafted into the Polish army. He was taken prisoner as the Germans conquered Poland, escaped, and was recaptured. After a prison camp and another escape attempt, he wound up in Flossenburg. Olek was constantly coughing from tuberculosis. Of all of us, he felt most hopeful that he would survive and return to his birthplace in the beautiful Tatra Mountains.

Rysiek, in his mid-30's, was senior to the rest of us. He was a chemical engineer and a man of few words. We learned somehow that he had been involved in the underground, and was caught. His body showed marks of recent torture.

The red-head, Yurek, was a robust young man. Until recently he had been an agronomy engineer working on the estate of an aristocratic family. His responsibility was to deliver to the Germans assigned amounts of farm produce. On his last deliveries, he was accused of withholding and hiding produce. He was imprisoned and sent to Flossenburg.

During the march we all stayed close together and supported each other. At my suggestion, after the guards herded us into a swampy field for the night, we formed a tight circle and sat on the bowls we carried with us. I insisted that nobody lie down on the wet ground after the day's march because it would be deadly. Sitting in a circle, we touched our heads to keep aware of each other.

We covered ourselves with the blankets we had carried with us from Flossenburg, to keep warm those April nights. Our most difficult task was to hold onto the blankets. Under the cover of night, some tough guys were tearing them off sleeping men and disappearing into the darkness. They had discarded their own blankets during the march to make walking easier. On the first night we lost one of our blankets.

All five of us managed to survive the first two days. The first to falter was Mietek. On the third day of the march, he showed signs of dehydration. Against my warnings, he started to drink water from puddles and ditches along the road. Almost instantly, he got diarrhea and fell back. That evening we were only four.

The next morning, Olek could not get up at the shriek of the guard's whistle. During the night, he had not sat on his bowl. He had stretched out on the wet ground of the marsh. He was making a strenuous effort to get up, but fell a few times. One of the guards saw this and shot him through the head.

After another tortured day of forced march, there were only three of us touching heads for the night circle, Yurek, Rysiek, and myself. We huddled together under a heavy snow shower. That night we lost another blanket to a night robber.

The next day we stayed together in spite of the rifle blows, swearing, and murder by the crazed German guards. On the fourth day of the march about noon, Rysiek started to fall back despite our urgings. No matter how hard he tried, he kept on dropping to the rear until we lost sight of him.

It was the last day of the march when a blow to the back of my head woke me up. I realized that I had fallen asleep while walking, and that I was not keeping my place in the column. The blow of the rifle butt was a warning to stay awake.

Soon I heard Yurek's voice and smelled the lingering aroma of coffee. Yurek told me that he had searched through the barrack hoping to find Rysiek, but there was no trace of him. Only the two of us were left.

I came back to my senses in liberated Dachau. The whistle called us for evening chow. The crowd was smaller than the day before. Many had not survived the first night and day after liberation. The death rate ironically had been substantially increased by the unlimited offerings of foods rich in fat.

Spooning the meal from my bowl, I listened to conversations around me. One fellow said that during the day, the Americans had brought the local German government officials from the city of Dachau. They had appeared in their Sunday best to present themselves before the new authorities. The last thing they expected was that they would be taken to the concentration camp to dispose of the many mountains of corpses.

Another group of Germans was taken by the Americans to the long lines of trains on the railroad sidings. They had to pry open the sliding doors of freight cars, from which corpses spilled out on their feet. In some of the cars moaning came from underneath the layers of corpses. People with signs of life were taken to the temporary field hospital which the Americans had established on the grounds of the camp. The Germans in their Sunday clothes had to work until sundown. They were ordered to report next morning and continue the cleanup. We were fascinated by the inmate's report.

Another inmate described how the camp commandant,

wearing white gloves, presented himself to the American officer in charge. With a stiff salute he reported the number of prisoners in the camp and stretched out his hand for a handshake. The American looked at him with contempt. He ordered two of his soldiers to take away the son of a bitch. The G.I.'s put him in their jeep and drove away. Soon shots were heard. Then the two Americans returned.

The news of the day included the suicides of Hitler with Eva Braun and Goebbels with his wife and all their children. It did not matter to me. I had no feelings about the suicides one way or the other. I was just very weary. I dragged myself to the bunk which I had by now all to myself. The barrack was almost empty. I dozed on and off.

I was again in Flossenburg. My dream was that soon after the two week quarantine ended, I got very sick with dysentery and blood discharge. I was so weak that one morning I could not join the labor column on the way to the stone quarry. I was sent by the block elder to the Revier, the barrack for the sick.

On the bunk next to me was a Czech inmate who struck up a conversation with me. He must have been well over 40 years old, very old for a concentration camp inmate. His completely bald head and steel rimmed glasses over the haggard face made him look 80. He was Dr. Strunc from Brno, Czechoslovakia, where he was a newspaper editor. He stayed in the Revier to avoid stone quarry work. Since Czech inmates held almost all administrative positions in the camp, they helped him. He shared with the Czech inmates the contents of packages which he would receive from his family in Brno. Only the Czech inmates in Flossenburg had the privilege of receiving packages from home. They were the camp's upper class and the envy of the other inmates.

In the afternoon, a German in uniform, accompanied by two inmates, was making an inspection of every bunk in the barrack. Learning what my problem was, one of the inmates brushed red ink marks on my forehead and chest, and continued their tour. I was paralyzed as I realized that this must be the end of the road for me. Warm tears ran down my cheeks. Then I felt that something was being put on my bunk. Opening my eyes, I was sure that my fever was responsible for the sight of a slice of white bread next to me on the bunk. I touched it and it did not disappear.

Strunc's eyes were on me. With a generous smile, he kept repeating, Don't worry. Everything is going to be all right. Just remember not to give up. Remember. Now eat this bread. It will make you stronger. Eat. Please, eat it.

Under cover of darkness, I sneaked out of the Revier barrack, and made my way back to my barrack.

At morning roll calls and in the marching column, I was standing up mainly thanks to the fellows on each side of me, who furtively supported me. During the day in the stone quarry, friends kept on looking out for me.

I remembered that charcoal was good for diarrhea, and decided to char my daily portion of bread. This took all the will power I could marshal. The bread we received in the morning was the main staple in our diet. I had stopped eating the noontime soup which was giving me serious bladder problems. Instead, I traded the soup for bread with fellows who preferred to eat warm soup.

For a full week, I subsisted on totally charred bread. The next week I charred only half of my bread, and toasted the rest of it. This made life a little easier.

After two weeks of this draconian cure, I started to feel better. The diarrhea subsided and I started to regain my strength. I became a legend among the inmates as the one who had conquered the deadly dysentery. I was fortunate that the kind Dr. Strunc had helped me at such a critical moment.

I awoke from my dream to loud, merry singing in the Dachau barrack. It was a kind of contest among different national groups, trying to best each other with their songs. It went on until late into the night. Without doubt, the Russians overwhelmed everyone else.

The next morning after breakfast, I had an urge to take a shower. In the shower barrack, a few inmates were enjoying the splashing of hot water. One fellow, obviously Italian, was singing arias from several operas in a powerful baritone.

I undressed, picked up a piece of soap, and got under a shower, this time without any fear that it might be something other than water. The pleasure was incredible. The long-forgotten luxury of hot water and rich soap suds was so pleasurable that I stayed there for a very long time, lathering myself again and again and producing enormous amounts of suds, just to rinse them off time after time. It was such a great feeling to be the master of my own time, and not expect a command to leave.

While I was rinsing off the last soap suds, I suddenly became aware of my body and was overtaken by a feeling of disgust. It was the body of a very old man, a bony skeleton covered with dried out, wrinkled skin that formed abominable looking, sagging bags on my chest, arms and thighs. I had a terrible aversion to the sight and got out of the shower. With more aversion and reluctance, I got into my filthy, lice-infested rags.

I rested on my bunk, depressed and agitated. I again tried to place recent events in some kind of perspective.

The Americans had arrived and liberated the camp on April 29, at about 4:00 or 5:00 o'clock in the afternoon. That was three days ago. It was May 1st. A shudder ran through me. This was my father's birthday. He used to joke that he was a socialist by birth. My mind wandered to 1943.

The Germans had shrunk the size of the Boryslaw ghetto once more. With the participation of Polish and Ukrainian police, thousands of Jewish men, women and children were murdered in a mass grave on the outskirts of the city. I was at the bedside of my father who by that time was mostly incoherent from starvation. Silently I wished that this man whom I loved so dearly would die. The sooner the better to escape the prospect of being dragged away, or shot in his bed. He died a few days later. His last moments were full of fevered anxiety for the safety of his children. The burial was arranged in a hurry, because the Germans and the Ukrainians liked to use such occasions to round up still more Jewish victims. There was no time for mourning and no time for self pity. As long as the instinct for self-preservation was alive, we had to run and hide with all the cunning available. The relentless hunt of the mighty German empire for every Jewish being drove on with no respite.

It was quiet in the barrack. The stronger men were outside in the warm sun. The weak stayed in their bunks. The sounds of their suffering were the only disturbance of the quiet. The loud shrieking of a man having a nightmare brought me back to the reality of liberation.

Now I was in Dachau. This was May 1, 1945, the third day of freedom brought by the beloved Americans. But what was the purpose of our having survived? A feeling of deep hopelessness brought cold perspiration to my whole body. How could I survive this liberation? Liberation for what? For whom? Was there anybody left worth living for? Anybody from my whole family? Anybody from all my friends and acquaintances? Anything from my world? Anything from cultural, religious, ethical, and aesthetic values?

Based on what I had been through and had seen, nobody and nothing could survive the systematic German murder which had been actively assisted or indifferently witnessed by our Christian neighbors. There was nobody to expect help from and there was no place to hide.

Suddenly, the question of where I was going to live now that I was liberated, became a load bearing down on me like a mountain.

THREE

Perhaps someone else in my family had survived, as I had. In the middle of my despair this hope kept returning.

The last time I had seen my wife was at the roll call square in the Plaszow Concentration Camp, at the end of October 1944. We had been brought there a few months earlier in a cattle car. The German soldiers had rounded up our group in the dense woods of the Carpathian Mountains where we were hiding in an underground bunker. At noon that day in Plaszow, all prisoners were unexpectedly marched from their work places to the roll call square.

In very tightly guarded secrecy, an unusually large transport train was prepared. Long cattle car trains were assembled on the railroad sidings around the camp in such secrecy that none of the inmates were aware of it. We had time for one last embrace, during which she managed to whisper between sobs, "Don't forget me." They separated us and took her to the train with her mother and sister. After the transport had left, it was rumored that all the trains had gone to Auschwitz.

Those last words of my wife stayed with me. I have often wondered what she was thinking the future held. Would I ever know?

After the transports had left, the Plaszow camp looked deserted. Most of the remaining prisoners were assigned to dig up many thousands of prisoner corpses. They had been buried at the camp when the Germans established it on the Jewish cemetery for the city of Krakow. At that time, it had not occurred to them that a day might come when they would try to obliterate the proof of their crimes. The unearthed corpses were burned day and night on open pyres. The stench and the fires in the dark nights turned the camp into an hellish inferno.

It became obvious to us that the transports and corpse cleanup operation were attempts to remove evidence of the mass murders, before the anticipated arrival of the Russians. Realizing this, we feared that the Germans would do away with the rest of us any day.

Instead, on a rainy November day, I was included in still another cattle car transport to an unknown destination. The train was going north. One day we passed through Dresden. What pleasure to see some of the destruction of that city. A day or two later we arrived at the Flossenburg railroad station. We were made to climb in formation up the road to the concentration camp located at the top of the mountain.

I stayed in my bunk reminiscing about the other members of my family. Desperately I search my mind for any indication of hope for the survival of anyone of them. The more I kept recalling the events which had taken place since the German occupation, the less hope seemed to remain. It seemed there was not a flicker of hope for a miracle of any kind.

Reaching that conclusion, I was at a loss as to how to face life alone in such a hostile world. How could I live among people who either had taken direct part in the mass killings, had aided the murderers, or had witnessed those horrors with indifference? The Christian world around us had watched with approval, or at best, with no concern. Murder and crime had become acceptable as long as they were directed against the Jews. Who could expect that with the end of the war, those same people would change and become decent human beings.

The future I had to face looked so ominous, that being liberated had become a source of new uncertainties and anxieties. Overwhelming bitterness took hold of me. Then anger. I felt as if I needed to smash something as big as the whole world to find relief. The worst of it was that these feelings could not be directed at anybody in particular. My desperate thought was that revenge might be the only purpose of my survival. But whom was I going to take revenge on? Was it going to be just anybody who was a German, Austrian, Ukrainian or Pole? Could it be done indiscriminately to men, women, and children the way they had done to us?

There was no imaginable punishment to fit the enormous crime that had been perpetrated against us. How could I even think of revenge?

Momentarily, I recalled an incident in the ghetto. Hunger was already rampant. One day, a lucky deal was struck with a Ukrainian peasant woman who dared to sneak into the ghetto to bargain a deal with the oppressed Jews. We traded a man's suit for a live chicken. Who was going to kill the chicken? Since nobody volunteered, somehow I was chosen and I couldn't get out of it.

So I made elaborate preparations. I found a stump, and carefully sharpened an ax. The strategy was that I would position the chicken so that its head would rest on the stump. Then I would strike quickly with the ax and chop off the head. I wanted to get it over with as quickly as possible but the chicken refused to cooperate. It put up a frantic fight, and would not stay quiet long enough for me to strike with the ax. My strategy failed and I gave up. I just could not do it. Finally somebody else took care of the matter. The remarkable thing was that nobody ridiculed me for not being able to kill a chicken, when killing of people on a mass scale was an everyday event.

Liberation hurt. I felt no joy or need to celebrate it. Instead, I stayed in my bunk thinking painful thoughts.

How was it, I wondered, that in all that misery of inhuman suffering, it never occurred to me to put an end to my life, one way or another? In my subconscious, there must have remained a spark of hope commanding me not to give in as long as I could avoid a violent death. It must be that the belief in the coming of the Messiah had its roots in the suffering of the Jewish people throughout the millennia. There had to be hope for a better future to give the Jewish people the strength to survive and overcome.

In the concentration camps, we kept hoping for the defeat of Germany even though every day we were facing our own destruction. We avidly followed every bit of news about the fronts and the Allied bombing of German cities. We drew conclusions colored by our optimism that the end of Hitler's Germany was imminent. Every day we survived brought us closer to the destruction of the German evil and our liberation. We lived for it.

Personally, I kept on hoping and believing against all odds that I was going to survive. This was my faith from day to day.

My mind wandered to the moment of our arrival in Dachau. We were sitting on the wet, cold ground waiting for the gates to open. My head was between my knees, my body contracted to a small bundle to preserve my body heat. On the screen of my feverish mind appeared the beautiful face of my little niece. I could see clearly the blonde hair and the big gray eyes looking at me, full of fear. That was how she had looked in the fall of 1943 when I had seen her last, just before her mother made the desperate decision to go into hiding with her. The Austrian garrison in our town was very zealous about outdoing the Germans in wiping out the Jewish population. Its members used refined cruelties which could be matched only by the Ukrainians. A Jewish mother and a two-year-old child did not have a chance unless they became like hunted animals.

The nightmare howl of the fellow huddling with me put an end to my hallucination. But soon I had another half-dream, half-delirium that let me mercifully escape the reality of the situation. This time my little niece ran to me with joyous laughter, and we hugged and kissed for a long time.

Still remembering my wonderful dream, I woke up. Now, I thought, liberation had made one part of my dream come true. I hoped with all my being that the other part of my dream would come true. It was so hard to think of a world with all my family gone. Such an empty world could have no purpose whatsoever.

Exhausted I fell asleep again. It must have been that not only the physical exhaustion but also the need to escape reality made me fall asleep again. There was no escape from nightmares.

This time my delirium took me back to 1941 when Germany attacked Russia. The day after the German army arrived in our town, the military commander gave the local Ukrainian population a free hand to stage a pogrom. The Ukrainians took full advantage. In the tradition of their national heroes, Chmielnicki and Petlura, they started murdering their Jewish neighbors. Men, women, and children were slaughtered, and Jewish homes were plundered.

I had hidden with a few other men in the attic of a house. We naively assumed that women and children would be spared, so they stayed in the open. As soon as they realized what was going on they ran for cover. For many of them it was too late. They paid with their lives.

Screams of fear and horror from the street penetrated the walls of the building. A mortal fear seized me. Every muscle in my body trembled out of control. I had once observed this reaction in animals entering a slaughter house.

The next day I was captured by a band of Ukrainians intoxicated with vodka. They added me to a group of Jews whom they had previously rounded up. They pushed us toward the center of the town with blows of rifle butts and shouted obscenities. There the local Ukrainian leadership added more abusive insults and cheers for our captors. I could not help noticing in a prominent place, the husband and wife couple who had been my teachers in the local public school. He had taught mathematics, and she Ukrainian literature. I had been one of their distinguished students. Now they were joining the mob in tormenting me and other Jewish neighbors on our way to death.

The Ukrainians took us to the basement of an office building. In the dirt floor there was a large, square excavation of
a mass grave. It was full of bloody, battered Jews. The air
was filled with the obscene shouting of the Ukrainian mob,
German soldiers' commands, and the moaning of the Jewish
victims.

On the rim of the grave lay one of the rabbis of our town.
A patriarchal figure, his face was bloodied where his beard
had been torn out. On his head were patches of blood from
rifle butt blows. His eyes, scanning the people in the grave,
were filled with deep sadness. Only his lips moved silently.
In all the frenzy around the grave, the tormentors did not
molest him.

We were thrown into the grave. Hardly anyone could
stand. Time and again the Ukrainians aimed their rifles
into the grave, and then, changing their minds, hit those in
the grave with their rifles.

This was going to be my grave, together with my fellow
Jews. I felt that I would scream and howl uncontrollably.
With all the will power I could muster, I took hold of myself
and managed to stay calm.

For some reason the Ukrainians refrained from shooting.
They seemed to want to prolong our agony by making us die
many times. Then a German officer shouted an order. The
Ukrainian hoodlums moved aside. The German ordered the
victims in the grave to get out and disappear. It was close to
4:00 o'clock. The Germans had decided that their work day
was over.

Later, I learned that several times that day that grave
was filled with Jews who were then shot. Each proceeding
group was forced to take out the corpses and then be shot
themselves. I lived only because I happened to be in the last
group before the Germans' quitting time. My body was badly
battered. I ran a high temperature and screamed in my
sleep for many weeks afterwards.

A nightmare scream in the barrack tore me out of the tor-
tures of my dream. I was drenched in cold sweat. It was

several minutes before I found time and place again.

The memories brought on by my dream stayed with me. I lay as if paralyzed in my bunk.

Why had I survived? I certainly did not deserve it more than any of those who had perished. They were all innocent people. Their only crime was that they were Jewish. Nothing else. Absolutely nothing else.

Now I was shaken by feeling guilty that of all Jews, I was one of the few who survived.

It seemed most improper to think that I was saved by a miracle, by divine power. This would imply that I had been specially chosen for that miracle. I had to reject any such idea as degrading to all those men, women and children who had perished. Why was I saved? The question would not go away. I was desperate for an answer.

A thought finally occurred to me. It was simple. I just was not killed. They missed me. I didn't succumb to hunger, cold, rain, snow, sicknesses, and slave work under inhuman conditions. I survived by a freak accident of fate. That was all there was to it. Nothing else.

The simple thought calmed me. I felt immense relief. No guilt feelings. There was only indescribable pain that I had lost my whole world. That pain was going to stay with me.

FOUR

It was one of the first days of May. I woke up to the familiar shrill whistle of the barrack orderly. It was still taking a while for me to realize that this was not the signal for roll call, but was for breakfast. The line advanced in an orderly fashion. So many unaccustomed foods were put on our plates. Scrambled eggs, fried potatoes, bread with butter. On the side was a kettle of coffee. Everybody was helping himself. It was still hard to believe that this was a real world, and not the horror of the concentration camp. I cleaned my utensils under a faucet in the washroom, and ventured outside.

It was a mild, sunny day. There was calm and peace in the air. I walked toward the main gate. The roll call square was full of inmates standing in groups. Makeshift flags of the many nationalities in the camp fluttered from the barracks and watchtowers, creating an atmosphere of freedom and exultation. I lost myself in the crowd. The many languages around me reminded me of the Biblical Tower of Babel. Expressions of happiness at having found someone, of the excitement of being liberated, and of sorrow over losses of family and friends could be heard all around.

I reached the Jourhous, the main gate. It was closed and guarded by American soldiers. A crowd of inmates gathered at the gate. Some tried to engage the Americans on the other side of the gate in conversation. What was the greater barrier between us at the moment? Language or the closed gate? One thing was painfully obvious. Nobody was free to leave the camp.

I became very angry. This was the only gate to the camp.

We, the "liberated," were locked behind it, still imprisoned in the camp. Did the Americans accept the German line that we in the camp were outlaws, and should not be set free? Why were no sick inmates taken to local hospitals? Why were they left in the camp? I resented the fact that our heroes, the Americans, were guarding us in the camp to protect the German population. They were protecting those hated Germans from the wrath of the camp inmates whom they abused, gassed, and cremated in the midst of their city.

A scrawny inmate in a worn striped prisoner uniform was letting off steam in broken German. His accent confirmed the marking on his blouse that he was French.

He was furious that we were not free to leave the camp. An older inmate, he had been assigned to different commands for all kinds of work in the city of Dachau. The camp was located in the city. The population could not avoid knowing what was going on in and around it. The city population smelled the daily stench of smoke from the crematorium. These people saw the unending lines of freight and cattle cars full of emaciated prisoners. They had seen gangs of prisoners being marched every day to all kinds of slave work in and around their city. They were a part of a system that lived and profited from the camp.

The speaker wanted to know why the Americans were protecting such people. The crowd listened, but there was hardly any reaction to his anger. Here was one lonely voice asking what should be done. No one answered. It was obvious that this was not a crowd to start any kind of protest.

I was disgusted. As I entered the street between the barracks, I was startled by the excited voice of an inmate in rags who kept repeating my name. At first, I could not place him. Then I recognized Moshe Meister, my barber since I was a young boy. How could I not remember this man and his shop? There, people had gotten haircuts and shaves and all the news about two local soccer teams. One was Polish, and the other, Jewish. Twice a year those two teams competed for placement in the regional soccer league. The com-

petition was always fierce. It was "us against them." The top
player on the Jewish team worked for Moshe.

Moshe and I embraced and looked at each other with un-
believing eyes. He told me that he was fortunate to have
survived, together with his son who was also in Dachau. We
exchanged information on our families. His wife and
daughter were on the same transport from Plaszow to
Auschwitz with my wife and her family. He knew nothing
more. Neither of us had much hope for their survival. We
talked long about people we had known in different camps.
We both promised to keep in touch.

Back at my bunk I was very restless. I went for a walk between the tall poplar trees that lined both sides of the
street. On my right the barracks were numbered one to 29.
On my left the numbers were from two to 30. The street ran
north-south with the roll call square at its south end. I
passed the disinfection barrack and the rabbit farm to the
right, and vegetable gardens to the left. I had never before
been in this part of the camp. Then, I noticed a big sign with
an arrow beneath it reading, *"Zum Krematorium."* The
arrow pointed to the left of the vegetable gardens. I wanted
to see no more, and turned back.

After the midday meal, I went outside to warm myself
under the bright sun in the space behind the barrack. This
was the so-called "neutral zone," about 10 feet wide. It ran
between the barracks and the wire fence. Prisoners had
been forbidden to enter this area under penalty of being
shot without warning from the watchtowers. Beyond the
wire fence was a wide, water-filled ditch, and then an
electrically-charged barbed wire fence, a high wall, and the
watchtowers.

The sight of the abandoned towers, the bright sun, and the
relaxed atmosphere had a calming effect on me. I stretched on
the grass and closed my eyes. The sun's rays warmed my body.
My good feeling lasted for only a short while. Anxiety and fear
came from nowhere. I had to keep opening my eyes to assure
myself that the towers were abandoned.

I sensed steps on the grass coming in my direction. Someone halted next to me. I opened my eyes and saw with relief that it was Anton, my block elder. He sat on the grass next to me. For a while he just looked into space, beyond the wall and the watchtowers.

He was in good physical condition, doubtless due to his position as block elder, which assured him enough food and saved him from the abuses of hard slave labor. He was known for his decent behavior towards the inmates in his barrack, so he was not removed after liberation.

After a while Anton spoke. He remembered me very well, he said. I was the one who could not wait to have my records changed to say I was a Jew. He wondered why an individual who had suffered so much for being a Jew was so anxious to be identified as a Jew again, even before the camp was secured by the Americans. What was my hurry? He could not forget my urgency and drive.

He told a close friend about this incident. The friend was Polish like me, and a priest. His name was Lech. He wished to meet me.

When we returned to the barrack, the kettle with the evening soup had arrived and the line of inmates with bowls in their hands was moving. The sight filled me with resentment. My irritation was that the rules of the German concentration camp were in so many ways still with us. I had thought Americans had an understanding of freedom and human dignity. How could they still tolerate the degrading ways of the Germans? On reflection, I had to justify the Americans' actions by the fact that fighting was still going on. That was more urgent than pampering liberated prisoners in the camps. Nevertheless, I was still annoyed at having to carry bowls strapped to our belts.

After the meal, I joined the crowd in the sitting area. Groups of nationalities gathered around individuals who had the latest news of the day. It was mostly about the gruesome cattle car trains with their cargoes of death camp inmates, and about the German city functionaries who had been forced to clean up the camp. In one group a Polish inmate told his listeners about a horrible discovery in a nearby forest. American soldiers found bodies hanging from trees. Somebody identified the hanged as inmates of our concentration camp who had worked outside the camp.

One group was very vocal. People talked in excited voices about their forthcoming return home to their motherland. To a man, they agreed not to wait a day longer than they had to. The Russians were the only exception. They feared that as prisoners of Germany they would be considered collaborators with the enemy, and might end up in Siberian labor camps.

I longed to be with loved ones again. Somebody started to sing a Slavic song full of sentiment and patriotism. The Russians took over and again overwhelmed all the others with their songs. Encores for the songs *Tchubchic* and *Black Eyes* were demanded and sung.

I wondered where my home was going to be. It could not be Poland any more, after what had happened to my people there. To me Poland was now just one tragic cemetery where my people were buried. Also, I was certain that the anti-Semitic hatred of the Polish people continued to exist with undiminished force. There was nothing to return to except Polish outrage that some of us had survived and might try to claim what used to belong to us.

With my whole heart I envied all the non-Jewish Frenchmen, Belgians, Italians, Yugoslavs, Greeks, Poles, and the rest of them. They had a country to return to and their families and friends to welcome them back. I feared the moment when the Dachau gate would open and I would be free to go.

That evening I decided that spending so much time in the bunk and letting nightmares consume me was not good. I had to get out and seek out the Jewish survivors in the camp. The next morning when I was about to leave, I had a visitor. It was Moshe. Without wasting time, he provided a chair for me to sit down, took out a worn towel which he wrapped around my neck, and gave me a haircut, arranging my hair as it had been in the old days.

From another rag, he produced a piece of gray soap, a brush, and a razor. With a bowl of warm water, he proceeded to soap my face. Then with the gentle touch of the master barber that he was, he gave me the smoothest shave in the world. My elation was dampened slightly by a few gray lice phlegmatically crawling on the towel. Neither of us paid them much attention.

In the tradition of his profession, Moshe did not stop talking and offered me cigarettes. He was given them, he said, as part of his fee for grooming the big shots in the camp.

Moshe told me what had happened to him. In October 1944 after the big transport from Plaszow to Auschwitz, he and his son were sent to the Natzwiler Concentration Camp close to the German-French border. They had registered as electricians on the advice of inmates. They were put to work in a large underground munitions factory. With a smile, Moshe remarked that whenever he had a chance his work had a barber's touch. He must have had been responsible for some surprises for the German soldiers.

Before he left, I asked Moshe how many Jewish survivors were still in the camp. He guessed that with all those still pretending to be Christians, there could be perhaps 2,000 Jews in Dachau. Something stirred in me.

On his way out of the barrack Moshe mentioned that he had been in Natzwiler with a chemical engineer who also posed as an electrician. This man was now in Dachau. Moshe was sure the two of us would like each other. Next time he would bring him along.

FIVE

It was amazing what Moshe's haircut and shave and the handful of cigarettes he gave me did for my well being. His catering to me, the personal touch of his grooming skill, reminded me of my dignity after all those years of degradation.

On the other hand, the constant itch caused by the multitude of lice on my body and in my clothing never stopped and I felt miserable. The suffering had worsened since I started to take showers. Either my skin had become more sensitive, or in the absence of fear and nagging hunger, the presence of lice came more to the fore. It was terrible to have to put on infested rags after the daily showers. No relief seemed to be in sight. I envied the inmates who worked in the camp administration and were wearing clean, even ironed prisoner uniforms. Ironically, those uniforms had a badge of distinction. During the last Nazi weeks when the influx of prisoners to the camp was massive, no striped uniforms had been given out. The prisoners had to remain in their lice infested rags. For us this had been one sign that things were not going so well for the Germans.

Early in the afternoon, Anton and another man came to see me. Like Anton, his companion also wore a striped uniform, and a beret of the same material. Anton introduced the man as his friend Lech, about whom he had told me. Anton excused himself, saying that he had things to do.

Lech looked very neat in his clean clothing. He had brown hair and a long, reddish moustache. His black eyes, set above a long, straight nose, were melancholy, but exuded friendliness. As much as I could judge, he seemed about my age. He was my height and very skinny, but apparently in good physical condition.

We shook hands, and he sat by me on the grass. We exchanged the usual information about the schools we had attended, the cities we had lived in, and other details of our backgrounds. I took a liking to him.

Since it was getting cool, we decided to walk toward the gardens. At the sign, *"Zum Krematorium,"* Lech asked me if I had seen the crematorium. He suggested that we walk there. On the way, he told me that the Germans had almost exclusively used Polish priests in the camp to build the new crematorium, which had replaced the old wooden one. Then the experienced priests were used to build the gas chamber and the SS dog compound. Lech added that the Polish priests were forced by the Germans to do this work in order to humiliate them. When I wondered if the priests had offered any resistance, I must have touched a raw nerve. Lech, too, wondered why the priests had not chosen death over building this factory for mass murder. Lech had been brought to Dachau after the new crematorium and gas chamber had been completed. He said he did not wish to judge anybody, but he could not help wondering too. But he felt he could not discuss the matter with the priests. They considered themselves martyrs, not to be questioned or criticized. He admitted that this caused him to feel shame.

The crematorium and gas chamber compound were located in a small woods just outside the camp. The crematorium was in a stone building. It contained two adjacent furnaces. Each furnace accommodated two trays on rollers. Corpses were placed on the trays and rolled into the furnaces where they were cremated.

On the wall above furnaces were gaudy murals in color, depicting happy youngsters sitting on the backs of jumping pigs. Under the murals a big sign proclaimed, *"Reinlichkeit is hier Pflicht deshalb Hande washen nicht vergessen.* Cleanliness is obligatory here so do not forget to wash your hands." I wondered who the artist had been. He must had been a cynic with a morbid mind.

We stood contemplating the unbelievable murals, the two furnaces full of human ashes and bone fragments, and the two trolleys covered with ashes and bones. Lech kept on crossing himself while his lips moved silently. I stood like a stone pillar, unable to move or show emotion. I only wished that I could cry a flood of tears to wash away the awful burning in my eyes. But I had no tears. My emotions were locked in, and there was no way to release them.

We moved on to the gas chamber adjacent to the crematorium. It consisted of the undressing area and the so-called "shower room," which had numerous metal shower cups mounted in the ceiling. They were actually traps through which Zyclon B poison gas was introduced after the Germans had hermetically sealed the room tightly packed with victims.

The gas chamber was about 16ft. x 16ft. x 12ft. high. It had one door made from a heavy steel plate. I could not help noticing that the heavy steel plate bulged toward the outside of the chamber. Only mortally desperate forces could have deformed such a heavy steel plate. I had to check my imagination. It produced pictures of the chamber crammed with people going insane at the introduction of the poisonous gas. The steel plate was pressed by those forces of human despair, and bulged.

In one wall of the chamber was a small window through which henchmen could watch what was going on in the chamber. Outside, there was still a plentiful supply of cans with the Zyclon B poison. The cans bore the name of the manufacturer,

A.E.G. FARBEN INDUSTRIE

To the outside of the gas chamber door were attached forms for keeping records:

Gaszeit, Time of gassing. *Zu*, Close. . . . *Uhr*, Time. . . .
Auf, Finish. . . *Uhr*, Time. . .

Below was the sign of a skull with two cross bones and a warning:

Vorsicht, Careful. . . G A S
Lebensgefahr, Danger to Life
Nicht Offenen, Do Not Open

Neither of us spoke a word as we left the place. We walked down the sloping platform which, Lech explained, was used to drag the corpses from the gas chamber to the crematorium. We walked into the large basement room of the building where numerous grinding machines were installed. They had pulverized the bones from the crematorium into fine bone meal which the Germans used to fertilize their fields.

From the end of the platform stretched a sizable plot. There under open sky loomed a huge pile of ashes from the crematorium. They were spiked with charred bone fragments.

That pile of ashes represented an uncountable multitude of people who had been murdered in cold blood in that place. The golden rays of the sunset were on the ashes, warming them in a fiery glow. The ashes seemed to quiver between the shadowed depressions and the illuminated surfaces.

I started to shake with fever. In my delirium, I could see an endless column of terror-stricken people, old and young, men, women, and children, terrorized by Germans in battle gear and their vicious dogs. The people at the head of the column were disappearing through the door to the gas chamber, followed continuously by more victims. A stream of burning ashes was gushing out the crematorium chimney forming a fiery arc in the pile in front of me. I could distinguish faces in the column. My teeth started to chatter. My whole body began to shake uncontrollably as I screamed and cursed the Germans for what they had done.

After a while, I was aware of Lech's voice, pleading with me as he was shaking my shoulders. He urged to return to the camp. My eyes burned terribly. Still, I could not shed any tears.

The next morning, Moshe came with the chemical engineer he had mentioned to me. His name was Yosef L. He was a man of medium height and heavy body frame. He wore a tight-fitting woolen cap of a dirty green color, and a worn prisoner uniform. The red and white stripe for his Polish nationality, and the yellow patch identifying him as a Jew were still sewn onto the left breast of his jacket. He had a friendly round face and smiling gray eyes. As we shook hands, friendliness seemed immediately to pass between us. Little did we know then that it was going to be the first friendship in our new beginning, and would last our lifetimes.

Yosef's story was not different from the average story of European Jews. In the early stages of the German occupation, he had lost his parents and his wife. He was taken by the Germans to the Plaszow Concentration Camp, built on the grounds of the Jewish cemetery in the city of Krakow. We discovered that for a short time during the summer and fall of 1944, we had been together in that place. In the fall of 1944, he was shipped to Natzwiler Concentration Camp. Under the pressure of the advancing Western front in early 1944, he was transported back to the central concentration camp at Dachau. Two days before the Americans arrived, a transport of Jews was assembled on the roll call square in preparation for a further transport. Yosef related to me bitterly how "our compatriots," the Polish inmates, searched all barracks for Jews who were hiding to avoid that death transport.

We cut short our conversation to go to the roll call square where the young American Rabbi Eichhorn had asked Jewish inmates to assemble. This celebration was to be international. The Jews from Poland, Russia, Hungary, Rumania, France, Italy, Czechoslovakia, Greece, Yugoslavia and Bulgaria assembled on that infamous square to celebrate together as a one people.

The rabbi, in the uniform of the American army, mounted the platform. In the absolute silence on the square, he started to recite in measured words the Kaddish, our ancient prayer for the dead. We repeated it word for word after the rabbi. Here and there, a heart-breaking sob erupted in the crowd. The chanting of the ancient Hebrew words went on like an unstoppable wave. Then the rabbi intoned the *El Molei Rahamim*. It was as if a dam had burst. In unrestrained sobbing, we let go of our stored-up grief. It took a while until quiet returned to the square. An inmate in a brand new prisoner garment thanked our liberators.

After the celebration, Yosef introduced me to Jacob S. and Mietek D., both also former Polish citizens. We talked about the situation of the Jewish inmates in the camp. Inmates of different nationalities had already organized themselves into committees which represented their interests with the new authorities. We agreed to organize a new Jewish committee which would speak for all Jewish inmates in the camp regardless of their nationality. To make it practical, we agreed to renounce our citizenships and declare ourselves stateless.

That same afternoon we got an appointment to see one of the aides to the camp commandant. We requested permission to form a Jewish committee. He was very polite and friendly, and tried hard to understand our problem. But he could not see why we would not want to return to our countries, our motherlands, as he called them. We were amazed how ignorant this young officer was of the history of Jewish suffering in Europe. Patiently, we described to him anti-Semitism, and the persecution of Jews in the countries of Europe. We explained that these were mostly the results of virulent, hateful teachings of the Church that the Jews had killed Christ and should suffer for it through all eternity.

We told the young officer that the Jews had been used as convenient scapegoats by the rulers of European countries, to divert the ire of the masses from the real issues of their own poverty and suffering. We described the collaboration of the populace with Nazis in the killings of the Jewish people.

Finally, we told him about Zionism, and the yearning of oppressed Jews of Europe for their own country in Palestine, the ancient land of their forefathers. He was sympathetic, and promised to present our case to the camp commandant.

Later that afternoon, we got our answer. The young officer apologized that he did not have good news for us. The commandant, Colonel Joice, he told us regretfully, had to decline our request because we did not represent a nationality. He did not want any complications from allowing us to form an organization representing citizens of different countries. We left his office in gloom. Nevertheless, we decided to meet again to find a way out of the situation. It occurred to me that even right after our liberation, we again had to face the ancient problems of being Jews.

At one of our later meetings, we decided to begin immediately the registration of Jewish inmates in the camp, to keep a record of the dying, and whenever possible, to identify the countless bodies before they were buried. The last could be done by noting prisoner numbers, if they were still on the bodies, and comparing them with the camp registry, which fortunately was not destroyed. Luckily, regardless of typhus and other sicknesses, some volunteers offered to help us in this difficult job.

One day, somebody got a brilliant idea about how to circumvent the commandant's political problem of a Jewish committee. We started with a new name: Jewish Information Office, Dachau.

We submitted our request for permission to form a Jewish Information Office, giving all the reasons for such an institution. To our surprise and joy, we were soon notified that our request had been granted.

We got a little office and started to function, officially representing the interests of the Jewish inmates in the camp. We also had all the prerogatives of the national committees. The Jewish Information Office members were Mietek Dortheimer, Yosef Lindenberg, Yoel Sack and Yakob Zylberstein.

SIX

Official recognition as the representative body of the Jewish inmates gave us the advantage of access to the offices of the American commandant and the International Committee of the inmates. This Committee was in charge of the camp offices and all the documents which the Germans had not managed to destroy. Until now we had to rely on the good will of the inmates employed by the Committee to occasionally let us look up the prisoners' names in registration ledgers. With the establishment of the Jewish Information Office, we gained the right of access to all documents.

This was important. We could now identify the sick and the dead. After we registered their prisoner numbers, we had to look them up in the registry to establish their identity. The exceptions were those who had passed through Auschwitz, where all inmates had their prisoner numbers tattooed on their left forearms. The only other concentration camp where the prisoners were tattooed was the one in Wieliczka, known for its salt mines. There, the Nazis inscribed on the prisoners' left arms, just about the wrist, only the capital letters "K.L.," which were no help toward identification. The corpses without numbers had to be buried without being identified. They were nameless, emaciated corpses.

We followed new burials of the deceased, and made certain that the graves of the Jewish inmates were marked with Stars of David. The rows of graves grew quite rapidly. Two to three hundred inmates were dying daily after liberation. Exhaustion, typhus, and the inability to digest food kept on taking their tolls. The fresh graves with rows of

49

crosses and Jewish stars next to each other reminded us that religion and nationality did not matter any more.

Keeping track of the sick was difficult. They were in barracks and the temporary infirmaries which the Americans had established in the camp. None of the sick inmates were transferred to hospitals in the town of Dachau, or in nearby Munich. We, in the Jewish Information Office, became extremely busy keeping up with the daily work load. We didn't want to miss any names. The registration of both the living and the deceased became an obsession with us.

Moshe visited me almost every morning to give me a shave. One day he was beside himself. A Christian chaplain, he told me, arrived in the camp and brought with him a Torah scroll, prayer shawls, and prayer books. The Jewish chaplain who had visited the camp a few days earlier had been dispatched somewhere else and could not bring the sacred items. He had asked his colleague, as a favor, to deliver them. Moshe could not comprehend it. Imagine a rabbi, in uniform but still a rabbi, letting a Christian clergyman handle Jewish religious objects including a Holy Torah! Those Americans, including the Jews, Moshe mused, seemed to be a different breed of people.

Moshe asked me if I remembered the *Kol Nidre* of 1944 in Plaszow and Rabbi Avigdor who had conducted the service that evening. His point was clear. There was a rabbi Moshe approved of.

Of course, I remembered that *Kol Nidre* night. We Jewish inmates in the camp had been fearful for weeks with the nearing of the High Holidays. The previous year, the Germans, on *Yom Kippur*, had rounded up most of the Jewish inmates, and had marched them out to the hill outside the camp which was the execution place. There they machine-gunned the Jews in full view of the remaining inmates in the camp. That event was seared in the memories of those who survived.

We feared that the Germans would repeat the massacre on the same occasion. However, on the eve of *Kol Nidre*, when the working commandos returned to the camp, no unusual movements of the guards could be observed.

As if on an unseen signal, the Jewish inmates started to congregate in one of the barracks. Even the camp elder and the capos cooperated. They set up watches around the camp to give a warning in case a German approached. The barrack was crowded to the walls. Many had to stay outside. I happened to stand next to the rabbi, Dr. Rabbi Abraham Avigdor, whom I had known from before the war. As I was valedictorian of the gymnasium in our city, I was introduced to him at our graduation ceremony. He recognized me and shook my hand with a sad smile. We wished each other the traditional *Shonah Tovah.*

A prayer shawl made its way above the heads of the congregants to the rabbi. As he put it over his head and covered his face with it, absolute silence instantly prevailed in the tightly packed barrack. With his eyes closed, the rabbi started to chant the *Kol Nidre* in a trembling, sorrowful voice. Pent-up emotions burst loose. A sobbing of desperation and helplessness filled the barrack.

There were no words, only the heartbreaking sobbing of the congregated men. From time to time, the rabbi's voice could be heard above the constant wailing as he chanted the *Kol Nidre* words for the second and then the third time. Toward the end of the third repetition, he, too, broke down. He could not pronounce the words anymore, but wept together with his tormented congregation of condemned people. All the time I stood next to the rabbi, I could hear in my mind the voice of my father chanting the *Kol Nidre* with our rabbi.

I assured Moshe once more that I would never forget that night of *Kol Nidre* and the *Yom Kippur* in 1944 in Plaszow. It had occurred shortly after the big transport to Auschwitz, when all the women were taken away and many of us lost our few remaining dear ones.

I met with Lech quite often after the visit to the gas chamber and crematorium. We usually found a spot in the camp's vegetable gardens where we could talk, away from the bustle of the barrack. Our first conversations were on Polish history and literature. Lech seemed particularly to enjoy those subjects.

One day Lech arrived carrying a pair of German army shoes. Triumphantly he handed them to me. He had noticed the tattered shoes I was wearing, he said. It took him a while to contact a Polish inmate who worked in the former SS warehouse. Lech asked him for a pair of shoes. The fellow would not disappoint a priest, Lech said with a smile. I put them on. They fit quite well. Both of us were pleased.

After Lech left, I held up the worn-to-destruction shoes. They had been given to me in Flossenburg by my young Russian friend, Misha. He had remembered me at the terrifying moment when he learned that he would be sent away on the next death transport. I couldn't part with them. On an impulse, I put them under the rolled up blanket that served as my pillow.

One day, three Jewish G.I.'s visited our Information Office. They had come to Dachau on leave to see with their own eyes what they could not believe was possible. They noticed the sign on our office, and came in before seeing anything else in the camp. One of them spoke broken Yiddish, which made possible conversation between us. When they were leaving to inspect the camp, I volunteered to show them around. After that, I filled in quite often as a guide.

One day I took two other young G.I.'s on a tour of the camp. When we came to the gas chamber and the crematorium, both of them became visibly disturbed. In front of the ovens, they started an excited exchange in short sentences. To my regret, I didn't understand what they were trying to say. One of them took off his soft soldier's cap, and dusted off one of the trays which was out of the oven. To my astonishment, he stretched out on the tray and his companion started to push him into the oven, stopping a few times to take pictures.

After the tray was pulled out of the oven, the young men

could not stop crossing himself and wiping perspiration from his face. Perplexed, he kept glaring at the murals of the clowning youngsters on the backs of the frolicking pigs. His friend was dusting him off with his cap. Both were silent while I showed them the rest of the compound. At the SS dog houses near the pile of human ashes, the two young Americans looked bewildered.

Visitors had different reactions, the most common being anger and disbelief. I was puzzled by those who picked up pieces of bones for souvenirs.

On the sunny morning of May 8, 1945, the loudspeakers announced that Germany had signed an unconditional surrender, and the war in Europe was over.

Celebrations started all over the camp. Groups gathered by nationalities for speeches and patriotic songs. Somehow alcohol found its way to the camp. Celebrations lasted until late in the evening. Unfortunately there were also some tragic deaths among the Russians and Poles. It came to light that they had somehow obtained ethyl alcohol and poisoned themselves with it.

In my conversations with Lech, the unavoidable happened one day. Talking about prewar Poland's sociological and political makeup, it was impossible for me not to be candid about the prevalent anti-Semitism and my personal hardships caused by it. I had been one of the very few Jews to be accepted at the Polytechnic Institute. There were three of us among 500 students. This constituted about one-half of one percent, while the Jewish population made up 10 percent of the people in the country.

I recalled the Jew-hating atmosphere in universities. Daily assaults against Jewish university students in the 1930's and the deaths of a number of them. I described to Lech the ghetto bench assigned to us, and how we refused to sit there. In protest, we elected to stand whenever we dared to risk attending a lecture.

All this was a reflection of the political, social and economic situation of the Jewish population in Poland. As

1939 came closer, the frenzy of Jew-hating intensified. The Polish nationalistic parties seemed bent on matching the Nazis in Germany. Hatred of the Jews had blinded them to the danger from their neighbor country for many of the past centuries. I was reminded of the verse by a great Polish poet who, referring to the misconduct of the Polish nobility in the seventeenth century, called the Poland of that period "the clown of nations."

Lech listened without uttering a word until I suggested that probably that Polish hatred of Jews gave Hitler and his policy makers the idea of choosing Poland as the place for the German system of extermination camps for the Jews from all over Europe.

This seemed too much for him to accept. Angrily, he retorted that Poland and its people had suffered immensely in World War II, and that it was unjust to blame them for the criminal excesses of the Germans against the Jews. Yes, he was aware of the attitude of many Polish people toward their Jewish countrymen. At first he hadn't paid much attention to it. The teachings of the Catholic Church blamed the Jews for the crucifixion of Christ. He had accepted this in blind faith during his growing up years.

Nevertheless, he was shocked when he had witnessed the violence of a segment of the Polish population towards the Jews under the German occupation. The willing cooperation of those people with the German enemy was revolting to him. It had made him rethink many things he once accepted, no questions asked. As a priest he probably was guilty of unorthodox deviations, in the eyes of the Church. Despite all this he could not accept my general accusations against the Polish people. He believed that the majority were good Christians, patriots, and decent people.

After an uneasy silence, Lech told me for the first time why he, as a small town priest, was arrested by the Gestapo and deported to Dachau. He had tried to help some Jews by sheltering them in his church. Then he became involved in saving Jewish children by placing them in the homes of trusted people. His activities became the talk of the town.

Lech had encountered resentment and scorn for being a "Jew lover." After his arrest, he learned that he had been denounced to the Gestapo by some people of his own parish, observant Christians who regularly attended church. Love and forgiveness should have been their guiding lights. How could they disregard those basic teachings, Lech wondered? Their hatred must have been immense to cause them to denounce their own priest. Although he had forgiven them, he could not stop wondering how their faith was so shallow that it was so easily uprooted.

I remembered what had happened to my new friend, Yosef, during the first hours when the camp was being liberated by the Americans. I told Lech how Yosef had come out of his barrack and cheered with others when the German guards were rounded up and put against the wire fence. Nearby was a Polish priest cheering with the others. Upon hearing expressions of happiness in Polish, the priest had turned to Yosef with a radiant face and an outstretched hand, uttering words of congratulations. But when he noticed the yellow stripe above the red and white patch on Yosef's jacket, he had withdrawn his hand and said, "There is one thing we Polish people will never forgive Hitler for, that he left some of you Jews alive."

One day the camp administration gave all inmates new SS uniforms. We tore off the insignia, happy to get rid of our lice-infested rags. It was weird suddenly to be surrounded by inmates in the green of the SS. But soon we were joking about it.

Still the gates to the camp locked us in. American military guards were posted around the clock. Over the gate were still the German words, "Work Makes Us Free." We were still not free to leave the camp.

Representatives of the Catholic Church were the first to arrive in the camp. Lech was quite sarcastic about it. Until the liberation, he said, the Church was silent on the subject of the hundreds of priests in Dachau. Now church officials showed up with huge supplies of food and clothing, making the priests the envy of all other inmates who continued to subsist on official rations in the camp.

A French delegation was one of the first among the nationalities to reach the camp. We saw heart-warming scenes of reunions as if the French inmates were all one family. Preparations for the repatriation of the French nationals began quickly.

Soon delegations arrived from the other Western European countries. Eastern Europeans took longer to arrive.

We Jewish inmates, watching these events, wondered when the gates of Dachau would be opened and we would be free to go.

Our work in the Jewish Information Office continued in a more organized way, since we had acquired two typewriters and some other office equipment. We knew that keeping records was very important, but we weren't sure how to make use of them. We watched for the right opportunity to get them out of the camp so they could be published.

One day a young American chaplain, Rabbi Abraham Klausner, came to see us and offered his help. When we showed him our work, he expressed full appreciation of its importance. He felt that our next task was to make our lists public, and assured us that he would find a way to do it. The man was full of energy. He inspired confidence in us.

By now Lech and I had become accustomed to meeting after the evening meal. We would either walk or find a quiet place to talk.

One day Lech told me that after the Church delegation had left, the inmate priests held lengthy discussions. The opinion of one priest, known for his independent views, disturbed Lech very much. The man said it was evident that Pope Pius XII considered it his foremost duty to preserve for the Church the treasures of the Vatican, and that he had not dared to antagonize Hitler with protests or interventions. But now the war had been over for several weeks, the shocking crimes of the Germans had become known to the whole world and still no condemnation had been heard from the Pope. Despite his unquestioning obedience to the Church, Lech said he was disturbed by his observations.

One day I met Yurek. He had become active in the Polish Committee and had moved to a block of mostly Polish inmates. We had seen each other only occasionally. He had made up his mind to return to Poland with the first repatriation group. So far, only the priests and a few Polish inmates had registered for repatriation. Others had decided to be emigrants, rather than return to a Communist Poland ruled by the dictator, Stalin.

I was glad about Yurek's decision to return to Poland. He would find relatives of Mietek, Olek, and Rysiek, and take them the bad news. Yurek reassured me that he was going to do his utmost to keep the promise we had given each other before starting the death march in Flossenburg. He had taken a burden off my shoulders.

Yurek was in a talkative mood. We sat where we had had our first taste of coffee after the liberation. One very painful Flossenburg incident stood out in his mind. On Christmas Eve only a few months before, the Germans marched us back from the quarry to the camp. As usual, the five of us including Olek, Mietek, and Rysiek marched in one file. Large flakes of snow covered the mountains and the road with a thick white blanket. On the mountain across the valley we saw the ruins of an old castle. Every time we passed those ruins, one of us would tell a story about a new cruelty of an imaginary German landlord who ruled the countryside. It was Mietek's turn. He spun a story in which the Hun led a raid over the mountains into Czech territory and committed terrible crimes. Mietek was actually telling a story of real atrocities by Germans when they conquered Poland in 1939.

We had arrived at the gate. The German guards had counted us scrupulously, and then shouted the order to march into the camp. Inside, close to the gate, a tall, well-illuminated Christmas tree had been erected. As we marched by the tree, we gaped at a ghastly spectacle. Beyond the Christmas tree there stood three gallows. Three bodies of prisoners hung from them, facing the brightly lighted Christmas tree. Yurek covered his face with both hands. That scene seemed to be burning in his memory.

I reminded Yurek about another abominable incident on that Christmas Eve. A group of Italian prisoners had been brought in that afternoon. After registration they were taken to the showers. Then, under beatings and being chewed by dogs, they were forced outdoors naked into the winter night. The guards forced them to run until the last one dropped dead in the snow. The rest of us in the camp had to stand at roll call attention until the end. Yurek remembered.

Another German show of contempt for religion and compassion happened about the fourth day of the death march. Our decimated human column was struggling under the guns of the German guards. It was go on or be shot. We were passing a roadside chapel near a village. A prisoner staggered out of the column, fell to the ground, and then desperately started to crawl toward the chapel. He managed to reach the foundation and embraced it, prostrate with his head tucked between his arms.

A guard, who saw him, halted a few feet from the crumpled man. A shot rang out, splattering brain and blood over the chapel with the Christ and Cross figure.

Yurek and I continued to sit in the darkness with these memories of bloody mass executions of men, women, and children for nothing else but being Jews. The Germans had been helped by Christians of other nationalities, relentlessly, all year around, for many years. The talk was too painful. We fell silent and embraced, two survivors of Flossenburg and the death march to Dachau.

One morning I got up with a cold and a runny nose. I could not believe it. For years I had been exposed to hunger, rain, snow, and cold. I had slept in wet rags which had to dry on my body. Yet I had never experienced a cold. Now, when my living conditions had become more decent, I got a cold. Somehow, I was glad. Had I started to shed the resistance of the hunted creature who was always on the run?

Another thing happened. I started to avoid contact with corpses. Before the war, I had considered my unwillingness to look at a corpse as a weakness, to which I did not like to admit. But during the war years, I had daily visual and physical contact with corpses. In concentration camps, with their bunks crowded, it was common to find out in the morning that the next fellow had died during the night. We would carry the body outside for the count of the living and the dead, and then hurry on to be subjected to our daily Gehenna.

It was a puzzle to me how my prewar sensitivity could return after all I had been through. Somehow, I was glad, but I decided to keep it as my secret.

SEVEN

The last days of May were full of events for the camp inmates. The first repatriation groups of French and Italians were assembled in truck convoys and left with songs and flag waving.

The Russians refused to be repatriated. Most of them had been fighting on the German side under the infamous General Vlasov, who had turned against his own country when victorious German armies were successfully invading Russia. After the Germans became unsure of the Russians' loyalty, they interned the Russians in concentration camps. Now they were afraid to return to Russia. Many Russian officers visited the camp. We learned that the Americans were under pressure to allow a forced repatriation of all Russian inmates, and were about to give in. The Russians started a riot and demolished their barracks. Some committed suicide. In spite of the protests, the Americans gave in and allowed the forcible repatriation to Russia and who knows what fate?

By the end of May, Yosef, Jacob, and I secured passes from the commandant's office to leave the camp for a few hours. We decided to visit the town of Dachau, and passed through the Jourhous gate in the early afternoon on a clear and sunny day. We walked past the former SS and administration camp to a wide asphalt road. This was my first time outside the camp as a free man. From time to time, I turned my head to be sure that no guard was following us.

The Lager Strasse, Camp Street, after a few hundred yards, joined the main road to Munich, the Schleissheimer Strasse. At the junction, we noticed a bar and decided to go in. In our pockets were a few German marks which an American officer who visited our office a few days earlier had given to us. In his car he had had a carton full of what he called "German junk money," and had given us some without even counting it.

Some Germans were drinking beer and talking in loud voices. This brought back unpleasant memories. We sat down at a table and ordered beer. Conversation had stopped when we walked in but it started again. To cover up our nervousness, we engaged in a lively conversation. We started to drink with deliberate calmness but after a few sips we felt the effect of the alcohol. We left without finishing our drinks.

The streets of the town were right up close to the camp. We were surprised to see private homes were so nearby. People were moving in all directions, preoccupied with their daily activities. What a strange feeling to be surrounded by all those Germans without fear of being harmed by them. After a while we had had our fill of the quiet German town with clean streets and beds of flowers and peaceful men, women, and children living their daily lives. We returned to the camp early. All I could think about was that those people lived so close to the concentration camp, and through all the years of its existence had profited by it and somehow had been able to enjoy life. How?

In early June, I secured a pass to go to Munich. There, the German Museum building had become a meeting place for survivors of the concentration camps. I decided to go there in hopes of meeting somebody connected with my past.

A small group of us inmates walked 12 kilometers through peaceful villages which seemed not to have been touched by the war. Going through the village of Allach brought back memories of my recent visit there at the plant of the car manufacturer, Bayerishe Motorwerke, B.M.W. I had been delegated by our Jewish Information Office to accompany an American army truck which would pick up the few remaining B.M.W. inmates and transfer them to the camp in Dachau.

Despite all my experiences in concentration camps, I was shaken once more by what the Germans had done. Near the impressive factory and office buildings, we drove to a stable-like hut, large enough to accommodate a few horses. It was crowded with three-story bunks, with hardly enough room to walk between them. No animals could be crowded so tightly, but men were. It was sickening. We gathered the few remaining skeleton-like inmates and left the B.M.W. plant as fast a possible.

Das Deutche Museum, The German Museum, was a magnificent building erected by the Nazi regime to glorify its proclaimed 1,000-year empire. The American occupational forces had requisitioned it for offices. A throng of military personnel rushed in and out. In addition, a swarm of liberated survivors from the many camps in the region milled around all over the building. Shouts of joyful recognition were intermingled with expressions of sorrow on learning bad news. On the walls, columns, windows, and doors were handwritten notes with the names, countries, and cities of origin and present addresses of the persons who put them up. Many papers also described whom the person was looking for. People moved along the walls, carefully reading every piece of paper.

I joined the others in reading but like most people I was unsuccessful in finding a single familiar name. At one column of the building, I met happily Moshe, the barber. He told me that recently, he and his son had chosen not to return to the camp, and were staying with others in a newly-formed refugee camp for former inmates. He had not located anybody. We promised to let each other know if we got any news.

To get back to Dachau, I hitchhiked a ride on an oxen-driven cart loaded with very long wood logs. The old peasant had me sit next to him and started a conversation. I munched on a piece of bread while the old man talked about the Americans zooming by in their flimsy-looking jeeps. He philosophized that at the end of our journeys, we all would arrive at the same destination, no matter how fast we had traveled. I dozed off as his monotonous voice unsuccessfully urged the oxen to move faster.

A few days later we were told by Chaplain Klausner that the list of Dachau survivors had been broadcast on the radio in Switzerland. That was wonderful news for us. The work we had done registering the Jewish survivors was starting to bear fruit.

Meanwhile, preparations for the first edition of Dachau and its branch camps, was going on feverishly. Chaplain Klausner was the driving force behind it. It would include articles for improving the status of the Jewish survivors. The first three articles stated:

1. No Jew need return to his native land.
2. Jews desiring to return will do so as soon as regular transports to their country are available.
3. Immigration problems will be handled on an individual basis by the Joint Distribution Committee.

A few days after my visit to Munich, someone told me that my youngest sister might be in a camp near the city of Stuttgart. We still needed permission to travel. I immediately applied for a permit to go to Boblingen-Kuppingen, near Stuttgart. The permit I got from the Military Government in Dachau was valid from June 18 until August 28, 1945. It pleased me that this was my first official document under the Military Government of Germany, rather than Dachau Concentration Camp.

Lech and I met before I left on my journey. There were rumors that the repatriation of the first Polish group would happen any day. Most likely, Lech would be gone by the time I returned from my trip.

I told Lech how much it had meant to me to know him and Anton after the liberation. It had taken no effort for us to overcome centuries of prejudices. They had not followed the Catholic teachings that I, as a Jew, was an eternal sinner for whom there was no hope of redemption. Living through an indescribable human tragedy, we had been capable of reaching out to each other for what we represented as human beings.

Lech took a while before he spoke. He said he had been
basically a same small town priest until we met. But he had
been fascinated by my insistence on making it known that I
was a Jew, at a time when I could hardly walk, and the
safety of the camp had not yet been secured. Then had come
our long series of discussions on Judaism and Christianity.
He had been fascinated that for me, the Bible was basically
the history of the Jewish people, with many wonderful
fables and allegories, that it was the code of laws and social
orders for the Jews at the time of their transformation from
tribalism to nationhood, that the Jewish core was the Ten
Commandments.

The historical background of Christianity, and the role of
the Jewish apostles in forming the Church, as I had
presented them, were a revelation to him. The fact that the
Church was instilling in Christians hatred of the Jewish
people by teaching the malevolent lie that Jews had killed
Jesus was now unbearable to him because he had become
aware of the deadly consequences, Lech said. He was very
pained to realize how one-sided and slanted his education
had been.

Darkness and quiet hung over the former SS vegetable
gardens. The hum of evening activities in the distance was
subdued. The sound of crickets seemed like thunder as Lech
stopped talking.

When Lech started to speak again, his voice was filled
with emotion. It seemed he had an announcement to make.
After all he had experienced during the German occupation
and in the concentration camp, he could no longer be a
priest. He had changed. He would still be a Catholic, but he
wanted a church which would return to the original Judeo-
Christian ideas of Jesus and his first Apostles. It must again
be a religion of love and commitment to the Ten Commandments with no room for hatred and persecution. The Commandments of "Love thy neighbor" and "Thou shalt not kill"
are absolute. There is no room for exemptions. Lech had
decided to become a *"kaznodzieya,"* a preacher, upon his

return home. He would travel all over Poland and teach the Testament in its pristine form.

Lech said he had been picturing the day when every Christian would face his Maker along with Jesus, His Mother Mary, and all the Apostles. They might ask if the petitioner had committed the deadly sin of hatred, and of hating and persecuting their Jewish brothers and sisters in particular. Even the Christian capacity for forgiving might be put to a trying test. Lech said he intended to ask this question of everybody on his return to Poland. His countrymen, with many strong family ties should understand the question, and hopefully, repent of the wrongs they had done.

But Lech felt full of despair for fear he was inadequate for such a mission. One day, while he was praying for guidance, it had occurred to him that I be persuaded to share that mission with him. Would I consider it, Lech asked in a trembling voice?

I was totally taken aback by Lech's request. I thanked him for his high regard for me, but explained that my plans did not include returning to Poland. For me the country represented a vast cemetery of the prewar Jewish community of 3,500,000 people, including my family and friends. If I went back to look for survivors, I would then leave as soon as possible.

We embraced warmly. "I hope that a future Pope will have your vision of the meaning of Christian faith," I told him.

EIGHT

On one of the last days of June, I left the camp wearing my SS uniform and the soldier's hobnailed shoes which I had recently acquired. On my shoulders was a soldier's knapsack containing a loaf of bread, underwear, and two new shirts given to me by the Joint Distribution Committee relief organization.

I was uneasy about striking out across the German land, but I was determined. There was no choice for me but to expect a miraculous reward.

Marching toward Munich, I soon caught up with a group of other inmates. Shortly an American patrol in two jeeps caught up with us. We must have looked suspicious in our uniforms. They herded us into the back yard of the nearest house, and examined our documents. The G.I. who checked my documents decided that I spoke Hungarian but that I would not admit it. I was asked to take off my shirt. They searched for the SS tattoo on my forearm. Satisfied that I was not an SS man trying to hide among camp inmates, they let me go with the others. I did not mind the ordeal too much, but it left me uneasy and scared of possibly being arrested as a German prisoner.

When we reached Munich, I started to look for the railroad station. The destruction from Allied bombing was unbelievable. Whole city blocks were rubbish. Most streets, however, had been cleared, and traffic, mainly military, moved freely. The railroad station was almost completely destroyed.

On the cleared platform was a group of women with packages. I was told that trains were not regularly scheduled, but that every day about noon, a freight train came through going west. Most of the time the freight trains stopped and let people on.

When I sat on a bench the woman next to me started a conversation. First, it was about people riding on the train to the villages to forage for food. Then searching questions about me. She was not surprised when I told her that I had started out that morning from Dachau and was looking for transportation to Stuttgart. Many inmates from the surrounding concentration camps now occupy former military barracks, she said. My uniform misled her. She took me for a released soldier who was returning home. This reminded her of her husband. The last news she had had of him was from the Eastern front, over one year before. She was on her way to the countryside to trade with farmers for food, so that her young daughter could eat properly.

A railroad employee announced that the train was delayed and would not come through for another two hours. The woman introduced herself as Frau Elsa and invited me for tea. She lived nearby. It would not take long to get there.

Her little girl opened the door for us. It was a small apartment in a partly destroyed building. While Frau Elsa was busy in the kitchen, I looked over the books on her shelves. One was Hitler's *Mein Kampf.* I was leafing through it when Frau Elsa came in carrying a tray with two cups of tea and a plate of biscuits. When she noticed the book in my hand, she offered it to me, saying that presently it might be better for her not to have it at home. I thanked her and put it into my knapsack.

Frau Elsa was a gracious hostess. She kept inviting me to help myself to more biscuits and tea. I was glad to oblige. Unknown to her, I was trying to figure out how many years had passed since the last time I had sat at a table and been served food. Her voice brought me back from my memories. She was telling me about the terror of the bombings, of running to the safety bunkers in the middle of the night, of destroyed homes, and the lack of food. She kept telling me what miseries the German people were subjected to during the war.

I asked Frau Elsa if she had known what was going on in the nearby Dachau Concentration Camp. No, she assured me, neither she nor her friends had any inkling about the cruelties which the Americans claimed they had discovered there. How about the slave labor, I asked? She had to have seen the emaciated men and women in their striped uniforms, in the city streets, being led by guards to work stations.

Perplexed, she said that everybody was sure those people were criminals or Jews. Then she realized that this had not been the right thing to say, so she tried awkwardly to cover it up with silly retractions.

Why, I asked myself, did she not have any curiosity about the conditions in Dachau? Did she already know? I suspected so.

Frau Elsa decided that it was too late for her to take a trip to the country that day. I thanked her for the hospitality, and the book and started on my way to the railroad station.

There was already a sizable group of people waiting on the platform when I returned. In a short while, we heard a whistle and the long train thundered into the station. It consisted of freight cars full of singing soldiers. The soldiers moved to make room for the waiting civilians. I managed to get into a car, and sat on the floor among the happy young soldiers. I soon found out that they had recently been released from detention prison camps in Italy. After a while I had had my fill of their boisterous stories relating to the war, the camps, and their future. I was resenting their German patriotic songs which were continuously repeated from group to group. A happy bunch of young men going home. Only exuberant happiness reigned in the freight cars. There was no mention of the war they had lost.

The doors of the cars were wide open. I remembered other freight car journeys of not so long ago. Those freight cars had

had been so crowded that there was hardly standing room. Men, women, and children were shoved in under the terror of German guards, helped by Ukrainian, Latvian, or Lithuanian henchmen wielding guns and whips. Then the doors were closed up tight and the compressed humanity agonized for days and nights in a hell which defied any description.

I took out the book I had received from Frau Elsa and started to read it. A dead silence in the car, and I lifted my head. All eyes were on me. I shivered. I was scared. Could they have found out about me? How? I was trapped alone in a train full of Nazis.

Finally, the soldier next to me said, "*Dumkopf*, idiot, are you crazy? Don't you know the trouble you can get into from this book? The Amis can lock you up as a Nazi, and goodbye to you."

Trying not to show my relief, I returned the book to my knapsack. The soldiers resumed their singing. I sat with my eyes closed, slowly regaining my composure.

Startled, I opened my eyes when a hand was placed on my knee. It was the soldier who had called me *dumkopf*. In a friendly voice, he advised me to get rid of that damn uniform as soon as possible to avoid unpleasant inquiries. Where was I from that I behaved like a naive schoolboy, he asked?

I told him the truth. He looked at me for a while, as if debating whether what I had told him was true. Then he pointed with his eyes to a man sitting nearby, and said in a low voice, "This is my lieutenant. Until about a year ago, he was in a concentration camp. Then they released him and ordered him to volunteer for front line duty to rehabilitate himself."

The lieutenant was a young man, but his features bore the vestiges of suffering. His dark hair had streaks of gray running through the middle of his head. He did not join in the singing. Strangely, I got the feeling of not being alone any more in that crowd of German soldiers. I relaxed and dozed off.

The screeching of the train wheels coming to a stop tore me out of my sleep. I was stricken with the panic of being again in a death camp transport. But the sight of the soldiers in the car restored my memory, and I calmed down.

The voice on the outdoor loudspeakers announced that this was Augsburg. The curfew hour was close, and everybody had to get off the train, the order said. Everybody was urged to find a shelter for the night, because the curfew was strictly enforced.

I was not worried. I'd find a room in the ruins of a bombed-out house, and stay there until morning. I started to walk out of the railroad station. A voice from behind me called, "Fellow, you fellow, wait." It was my acquaintance from the car. He introduced himself as Hans, and then introduced me to the lieutenant, Herr Helmut C. We shook hands. Helmut told me that if I wished, I was welcome to join them for the night, wherever it would be. Dusk was coming fast. I followed the two of them down eery streets between ruins of destroyed buildings. Hans was scouting for a shelter. Helmut seemed to have full confidence in his orderly's ability. We stopped at the ruins of an apartment building. Half of it had survived a bomb and stood as if a surgeon's knife had performed a delicate operation, separating it from the part which had been destroyed. On some floors, only parts of rooms had survived, exposing bedrooms, dining rooms, kitchens, and bathrooms. Many pieces of furniture were still in place.

Hans climbed into the ruins to explore. Soon we heard his voice urging us to climb after him to the second floor. By the time we got there, Hans was busy exploring the place. It had been a nice apartment before the bomb hit. Only the kitchen and one bedroom had survived the destruction. Soon we heard his excited voice letting us know that Americans must have been here before us. He had found cans of conserved meat and fruit and a can of powdered coffee. Then came the real bonanza. In one of the cabinets there was a bottle of French wine, a bottle of cognac, and American cigarettes.

Hans got busy preparing the meal. Helmut let his orderly do all the work. The end of the war had not changed the old German army relationships.

I lay on the floor and took off my shoes so my aching feet could relax. Helmut followed suit. His eyes were on me when I lifted my head. They showed friendliness and curiosity. We rested in silence. A thought came into my mind that I must be on guard all night. Would these two Germans kill me in my sleep just for the sport of it?

From the kitchen came Hans' voice announcing that the meal was ready. Helmut got up and invited me to join them. There were three plates and three wine glasses on the kitchen table. Hans served with the air of an experienced chef. He poured two glasses of wine. Only after Helmut asked him to did he fill one for himself. The cans provided meat, vegetables, and fruit from which Hans made a royal meal.

The wine, food, and the coffee worked wonders. The three of us were fully relaxed. Helmut's, "This was really good," caused Hans' face to radiate happiness.

Hans prepared two sleeping places on the floor of the bedroom. I wondered what had compelled him to include me in his hospitality. He lay down on the kitchen floor, and was sound asleep in no time.

With the cognac, two glasses, and a few packs of cigarettes between us, Helmut and I made ourselves comfortable on the floor. I started the conversation by remarking on Hans' kindness. "He was a simple farm boy," said Helmut, "who did not get poisoned by Nazi propaganda." Luckily for both, he had been assigned to Helmut as orderly. The farmer boy's innocence survived the rowdiness of the army.

Helmut refilled the glasses and we lit new cigarettes. "I know," he said after a while, "that you were in Dachau, and you know from Hans that I was in Oranienburg for over a year. Your German is flawless, but you are not German. Where do you come from? For what kind of sins did they get you to take up residence in Dachau?" He was born and had grown up in Frankfurt, where his father was a well-known builder. He himself was an architect, and had joined his father in the business. The firm was engaged in construction so important to the war effort that he was exempted from military service. At some point difficulties piled up. Shortages of materials caused projects to be late or have no prospect of being finished. Helmut was critical of Nazi Party rule and foolishly did not hide it. The firm was blamed for negligence. When an official accused him of sabotage and aid to the Communists, he exploded with derogatory remarks about the Government. The Gestapo arrested him that same day. He was accused of being a Communist, and was tortured to admit it. He resisted. One day, stripped naked, he was bound to a bench. A vice was applied to his testicles until he fainted. When he recovered he was in a moving van with several other men. They were brought under heavy guard to the Oranienburg Concentration Camp. About a year ago he was ordered to the office of the camp commandant. He was told that he had been drafted into the army to serve in a special combat unit and rehabilitate himself.

After a few weeks of intensive training, he was shipped to Italy and thrown into the hottest battles against the advancing Americans. He was given the rank of lieutenant when the corps of officers became seriously depleted. Still the stigma of the former concentration camp inmate followed him and he remained under suspicion until the end of the war.

The cognac was getting lower in the bottle, and the ashtray was filled with cigarette butts by the time Helmut had finished his story. We remained silent for a long time. We refilled our glasses and lit new cigarettes. It was my turn. By now I was at ease with the young German. His friendly attitude and the story of his bad fortunes inspired my trust. I felt like opening up to him.

I started by telling Helmut that I was a Jew, a native of Poland. Then I described what had happened to the Jewish population immediately after the German forces occupied the country. The wild pogroms staged by the German military in partnership with the darkest elements of the Ukrainian population. The terror of being stripped of all rights and dignity, and becoming an object open to abuse, including death, by anybody in the population.

German soldiers and officers had behaved like the bloodiest Huns of the past. They had come to the ghetto to satisfy their most gruesome lust for torture. Sometimes they plunged a bayonet into the swollen belly of a pregnant Jewish woman, or fired bullets aiming at the crotch of a young girl. A favorite sport of young German soldiers was to throw Jewish babies into the air as target practice for their comrades. Gruesome games of picking up Jewish babies by their feet, and smashing their heads against a wall, were accompanied by the fiendish laughter of the amused Germans and Ukrainians.

It was not Helmut any more whom I was telling all those things to. I didn't care who it was. Those nightmares lingering in my mind like embers in ashes, became live flames, and there was no way of containing them. The gates to the painful past were open. All those pent-up memories came forth in a gushing flood.

"When the horrors of the extermination camps become known to the world, people will find it impossible to believe that those things really happened," I told Helmut. I must have talked for a very long time. When I saw Helmut's face, his eyes were full of horror.

The first rays of the new day appeared through the shattered window. We stretched on the blankets that Hans had prepared for us. I was falling asleep when I heard Helmut say, "All Germans, we are all responsible for those despicable crimes. There can be no redemption for us. I do not regret that I won't be able to father any children. Our new generations will have nothing but contempt for their fathers when they will learn what they did in the name of building a German empire to last 1,000 years. This will be a terrible burden for them to live with."

I woke up to the smell of coffee. It was late morning. Hans had the breakfast ready. It was not long before we were on our way. We found the main street, and decided to hitch-hike to Ulm. It was difficult because there were many returning war prisoners to compete with. Finally Hans succeeded in stopping a crowded truck, and we got on. There was standing room only. We swayed in unison to every turn the truck made.

Ulm was in ruins like Munich and Augsburg, but its famous cathedral stood intact in the midst of the destruction. It must had been the skill of the Allied reached the center of the city, we all had to get off. We made our way to the railroad station to ask whether there was a chance of getting on a train going West.

Helmut, Hans, and I stuck together. I attracted unwanted attention because of my uniform, and heard remarks about my being stupid walking around like that.

We were lucky. Soon after we got to the station, a freight train pulled in. It was going to Stuttgart. We got on and set-tled in the doorway of a car filled with crates and a small group of soldiers and civilians.

Hans told us that in the station he had overheard people saying that the Americans were going to continue to push east, and drive the Russians back to their old borders. Most people felt it was logical. Somebody supposedly had secret information that it was going to happen.

I had my doubt that such a thing was possible. The Americans were not going to turn against their ally. Such an idea seemed to me like wishful thinking. I could see that Germans feared the wrath of the Russians for the destruction Germany had inflicted on Russia. Now the Germans ex-pected to be protected by the Americans.

We sat watching the countryside and listening to the monotonous noise of the train wheels hitting the gaps be-tween rails. I was about to reach for the book in my knap-sack when Helmut started to talk.

"Last night," he said, "I felt guilt when you were telling

your story. I never joined the Nazi party. I led a very comfortable life until they grabbed me. Yes, I was aware of what was going on in the country, but like the rest of my family, I decided not to get involved. When I learned about the slave labor used in our industries, I found justification for it in the demands of the war. I'm ashamed to admit that I didn't go to the trouble of finding out the whole truth.

"In my circle of friends, we criticized our government and its policies, but we were not concerned about the concentration camps, slave labor, and German activities in the occupied countries. The only things we cared about were the fortunes of our fatherland. Only after my battle with the Gestapo, and my experience in the concentration camp, did the truth of the criminal regime we had created dawn on me. If I had not seen it with my own eyes, I could never have imagined such horrible depravity.

"By then the thing that mattered most to me was my own survival. In no time, with the help of other German prisoners, I was getting all the small privileges granted even in that place to members of the superior race. I got a job as clerk, had enough food, and never had to go out with a commando to do physical work.

"When they made me join the army I dutifully complied. I was a good soldier, fighting in the hopeless battles of a lost war. It didn't occur to me that I was fighting to prolong the rule of the party I held in contempt. With my false sense of duty, I was not thinking how the war was sacrificing the lives of the very young and very old who had been inducted to fill the gaps in the front. I was just once again a German doing his duty. I am deeply ashamed now of being so rigid, so thoughtless in what I have done."

The train was approaching the temporarily reconstructed bridge over the Neckar river. It was very narrow, just wide enough to accommodate one pair of rails. For us, sitting with our feet dangling out the door, the bridge disappeared under the train. The train seemed suspended high in the air between the two banks of the river. It was scary. Suddenly it occurred to me that any of those Germans in the car could have pushed me out into the air and the river.

Instinctively, I moved close to the door frame to a position where I had a partial view of the inside of the car, and my shoulder was against the wall.

We were approaching the end of the bridge and entering the Stuttgart railroad station. Helmut wrote his address and telephone number on a piece of paper and handed it to me with a request that I be in touch with him. Then he took out a billfold and offered me a sizable wad of marks, saying that I would need it on my trip. Politely, I said, "No."

In the station, I warmly shook the hands of Helmut and Hans, and jumped off onto the temporary platform. I turned around, and we waved to each other.

Helmut had told me it would take about two hours to reach my first destination. That would be well before curfew. Without wasting time, I got out of the railroad station and headed for the streets of Stuttgart.

NINE

Stuttgart was badly damaged like the other cities I had a chance to see. But I walked briskly and did not pay much attention to the ruins. My hobnailed shoes made a loud clatter that reverberated in the ruins of the houses. My feet walked to the beat of the echo.

On one street, I saw a barber shop and walked in to get a haircut and a shave. The proprietor was alone and invited me to sit in the barber chair. He tried to make conversation, but I said very little. He assumed that I was returning home from a prison camp, but my uniform puzzled him. He refused to take money.

When the barber confirmed that my directions were correct, I got moving. Several women warned me to avoid the area where the French had their headquarters. The French occupation personnel were reported to be tough with Germans. My uniform could invite trouble for me.

The sun was dropping in the sky. The hour of the curfew was drawing near. I had to find a place for the night. Seeing a house that looked modest compared to others, I knocked on the door and asked the woman if I could spend the night in their barn. She scrutinized my face and uniform and then called out into the house. An older man came out, looked me over and asked me in. The table was set for the evening meal. He invited me to join them.

During the meal the couple discreetly did not ask questions, and I volunteered no information. The conversation stayed on neutral subjects during the whole meal. The couple showed me to a room with an old-fashioned bed, white pillows, and a blanket in a white sheet. I stood there for a long time, trying to believe that it was for me to sleep in. For so many years, including the time since liberation in April, I had slept on the ground, the floor, or in a hard bunk. I hesitated before I got into that bed. I didn't think I could fall asleep in that clean, white luxurious bed.

Determined, I undressed and slipped naked under the cool cover. It was a long time before I fell asleep. Memories from the past were too disturbing. Tiredness finally took over. My dreams were vivid about home and family.

When I woke up, it was hard to accept that they had only been dreams. A hollow feeling of emptiness wouldn't go away for a long time.

In Stuttgart, I found the office of the Central Polish Committee for the area. The two small rooms were meagerly furnished. From the only man in the office, I learned that the Occupation authorities had established Displaced Persons camps in Ludwigsburg, Vaihingen and Boblingen. In those D.P. camps lived the former prisoners of the many local camps which had supplied slave labor to the industrial plants around Stuttgart.

My new mission became to visit those camps. After reading lists of inmates in the camp administration office, I mingled with the people, and looked for somebody I might know. The inmates were of many nationalities, most of them Russians and Poles. Very few Jews were in those camps. Before leaving, I placed on the bulletin board a note with my name, the name of my sister whom I was looking for, and my address at the Jewish Information Office, former Dachau Concentration Camp. I would eat meals and stay overnight in the camp where I happened to be at the end of the day.

It was already the end of June, which meant that the inmates of these camps had been liberated about three months earlier. Many of them still lingered in the camps under very primitive conditions. They no longer had to perform as slave laborers, but the idleness was devastating for their morale. UNRRA, the United Nations Relief and

Rehabilitation Organization, administered the camps and provided food. But there was no real attempt at any kind of rehabilitation program to prepare people for life after the camp. Unhappily, this seemed to be the established pattern in almost all the D.P. camps.

After several days of unsuccessful searching, I returned to Stuttgart and once more visited the Polish Central Committee. The same man was in the office, giving information to two young women about repatriation to Poland. While the two were filling out forms, he asked for the results of my search. I told him about my failure and asked permission to place a slip on the bulletin board with the message like the one I had left in the camps. Then I explained that I was returning to Dachau, and intended to travel to Poland in search of survivors in my family. I was hoping for some provisions to eat during the trip to Dachau. The only thing he could give me was a loaf of bread.

The two women stopped writing, and listened intently to our conversation. When I left the office, they followed me and asked if they could go with me to Poland. I explained that I had some obligations first in Dachau, and didn't know how long I'd have to stay there. Then they asked if I could take names and addresses of some people whom I would notify about their whereabouts.

The two women introduced themselves as Ala and Sofia. Ala had a dark complexion and raven black hair. Her brown eyes sparkled. She was full of lively gestures and quite talkative. Sofia was quiet. Her hair was ash blonde and her gray eyes projected deep sadness. She didn't say much, but listened very attentively.

It was about noon. The ruins and the sidewalks radiated intense heat, making it uncomfortable on the street. We walked into the shade of a nearby orchard to continue our conversation. I got the impression that the two were trying to establish my identity. My uniform could not have made them doubt my Polish origin. Our conversation had made it clear that I was from Poland. Suddenly it crossed my mind that these two were Polish Catholics who suspected that I was hiding my Jewish identity. Angrily, I accused them of not having the decency to ask openly if I was Jewish, if that was what they were after. Yes, I said, I was Jewish.

What followed, I could hardly believe. Both women became hysterical and sobbed without restraint. They confused me. I didn't know how to react. What I did was to wait until they calmed down. Then I waited some more for an explanation.

Finally, they spoke. Both were Jewish. After buying phony Catholic birth certificates in Poland with their last possessions, they deliberately exposed themselves to a street abduction, one of many which the Germans used to deport people for slave labor in Germany. They met each other for the first time in Germany. Each had chosen the same risky method of escaping the death camp trains and had succeeded.

Although the French had occupied their area of Germany about three months before, they continued to live under their religious disguise. The reason was that they did not believe that any Jews at all could have survived the German death camps. They continued to work for their German proprietors. They did not dare to reveal their Jewish identity, even to the French and Americans. Both were still known as observant Catholics.

The hot July sun kept the streets deserted. We spotted a beer joint and walked in. They continued their stories. Sofia had been assigned to work in a beerhouse, and Ala in a central warehouse for grocery products. Both had to work from daylight until late in the evening. Their only "pay" was food, and a bed in the servants' quarters.

From time to time Ala and Sofia looked at each other, at me, and then again at each other to see the happy smile on their faces. Obviously, in me they had found somebody they could feel close to. They could not contain their happiness.

The women continued their story. The two German families to whom they had been assigned were good friends.

So Ala and Sofia met and began to see each other on Sundays. As time passed they started to notice in each other subtle indications of some kind of bond between them. Neither remembered just when it had happened, but finally they each discovered that the other was Jewish. Their burdens became easier to bear.

The women suggested that I stay overnight in their village, where they could secure me a room in a lodging house. I gladly accepted.

It was a long walk to Boblingen. We arrived late in the afternoon. After introducing me to her proprietress, Sofia walked with me to the rooming house, a two-story building with single room accommodations on each floor. At one end of each floor there were common washroom facilities.

After a long hot shower, I fell asleep, oblivious to the world. I had a wonderful dream about being with my wife, Doncia. We embraced and hugged. She caressed my cheeks and hair. The dream was so vivid it bordered on reality. The caressing continued and assumed a physical quality as I emerged from sleep. Then I felt a real person next to me. Slowly I opened my eyes.

Sofia was sitting on the bed next to me, caressing my head. She greeted my sleepiness with a warm smile. I had slept for a long time. It was night already. Only a table lamp provided light in the room. Sofia stayed with me all that night.

Regaining my manhood was a miracle. It gave me a special feeling for this young Jewish woman, who was so happy to learn only hours before that I was a Jew who had survived.

During the years of terror and hunger, the sex drive had disappeared from our life. Men became impotent, and women ceased to menstruate. Nature itself put on hold the means of procreation, under such conditions of bare existence.

Sofia and I talked about our experiences from the start of the war. She had been married for only a short time when her husband was murdered by Ukrainian neighbors at the onset of the war. She told me about other tragedies that had followed.

Sofia left at daybreak, not wishing, as she put it with a smile, to scandalize her middle class German proprietress. In Boblingen, I found out that the French were completing their pullout from the area, and would be replaced by Americans.

A few Americans I met were of Polish or Ukrainian extraction. They spoke bits of the languages of their immigrant parents, which was helpful in communicating. Their favorite activity was to photograph everything in sight with their newly acquired cameras. They snapped me in the SS uniform with an American army cap on my head.

Following the wishes of my new lady friends, I did not disclose my Jewish identity. They were not ready to cope with that while they were still in Boblingen.

It was time for me to leave. I promised Sofia that I would keep in touch, and would let her know if I learned of any Jewish survivors in her vicinity. Our American friend, Lieutenant Ludek, offered me a lift to the railroad station.

When he came to pick me up, there was Sofia next to him in the jeep. She gave me a list of names and addresses of people to be contacted in Poland. She was sad but composed. At the impatient tooting of lieutenant's horn, we embraced once more. She managed to whisper, "What happened has been like a miracle. I am still in kind of a daze."

During the ride, Ludek told me how concerned he was about the boys and girls who had been brought forcibly from Poland to Germany to work in factories and on farms. Lately, they had been intoxicated with their freedom, and were enjoying being fed and not having to work. Very few were planning to return to Poland. Many were involved with German women, who had welcomed them as substitutes for their missing men. Only months ago, punishment for a foreign worker having an affair with a German woman had been death by hanging, and for the woman, ostracism by her peers. Many young Polish women seemed to enjoy their freedom away from home, and chose to stay in the D.P. Camps. The idle life in those camps was demoralizing. If only more of them were like Ala and Sofia, Lieutenant Ludek mused.

One day in the rooming house, two young fellows who lived there overheard me speaking Polish with Sofia and invited us for a drink. Their room was full of half empty suitcases, dresses, shoes, all kinds of food, and bottles of hard drinks. To our surprise, we learned that they engaged in what they called "organizing suitcases" on trains. They had been boarding trains and traveling between various cities. When the train stopped at a station, they would terrorize the passengers by pushing, and cursing. In the melee, they grabbed choice luggage and disappeared. That was their idea of taking revenge on the hated Germans. They bragged that they were living very well on the booty. The sad part, Lieutenant Ludek and I agreed, was that the young boys were convinced that what they were doing was perfectly all right.

We stopped at the station for a while. Ludek thanked me for telling him about the two boys. He had in mind to talk to them before they get into trouble with the authorities.

After several hours' wait, a long freight train arrived at the station headed east. Only one open gondola car was available to the waiting group of civilians. Soon after we had left Stuttgart, it started to rain. Most people had raincoats and umbrellas to shield themselves. The woman next to me invited me to share her umbrella. We used the forward wall of the car to shield us against the rain, which was intensified by the moving train.

It was dark when the train pulled into Nuremberg. We were ordered to leave the train and the station. When we reached the street we were rounded up by M.P.'s and taken to their post. We had broken the curfew, one M.P. announced in quite good German. I showed him my pass from Dachau. After a stern interrogation, I got a chance to explain that the whole group was on the street during the curfew time only because the train had arrived late. Then a heavy-set M.P. who spoke a mixture of Polish and Ukrainian questioned me further. Somehow he managed to understand my story. Once he was convinced that I was telling the truth, the M.P.'s took all of us to a nearby school, and put us up in the spacious gym. I was a celebrity with the group. The young woman who had shared her umbrella felt important and stayed at my side.

We were given two blankets each for sleeping on the floor of the gym. A big kettle was brought in, and hot soup was distributed together with some bread. It felt good after the wet ride in the open railroad car.

At the end of the room, two middle-aged men were noisily arranging a table and two chairs. They called for attention, and announced that they were German survivors of the Buchenwald Concentration Camp. After liberation, they had written their memoirs of Buchenwald. They wanted to take advantage of the evening ahead, and share their experiences.

The two men took turns reading about the conditions in the camp, the roll calls that lasted for hours in all kinds of weather, forced labor, hunger, lice, cold, and unending terror. They read about prisoners from many lands who had been denied any humane treatment and had been left at the mercy of the German guards, and the capos recruited from the worst criminal elements. Jews and Gypsies had been slaughtered on a mass scale. On and on, the two of them continued. The captive audience listened in grave silence.

A man's voice from the audience interrupted the reading, "We had no knowledge that such things took place. We had no idea whatsoever." Other voices joined in, "We did not know. We had no idea."

The younger man on the podium lifted his arm for silence, and said in a accusing voice, "So far, wherever we have been in Germany, we have been getting the same reaction to our story of the inhuman cruelties committed in the concentration camps. You, too, claim that you did not know. But this is not possible. It has the same hollow ring of a conspiracy. There were so many of those horrible camps in the country that it was impossible not to know about them. People who lived near the camps and saw the trains filled with dying, human cargoes, who could smell and see the smoke belching from the chimneys of the crematoria, try to say that they had no idea what was going on.

"The country seems to have unified itself around the idea of disclaiming any knowledge of the inhuman crimes committed by husbands, sons, and yes, also by many of our women. But the world cannot and will not believe this obvious lie. Hitler and his small Nazi party had to have the support and collaboration of our whole nation for all these misdeeds."

An enraged voice rang out from the audience. "Shame on you. That's not how a German should speak. We must stick together against a world which combined even with Communist Russia to defeat us. No wonder you were locked up during the war. Shame."

The eyes of the girl next to me were full of tears. She implored me to tell her if any of this was true. By overhearing my conversation with the M.P., she knew that I had been in Dachau.

I told her that what she just had heard was only a meager description of what had gone on in the concentration camps. But I gave those two men full credit for trying to give a picture of things so horrible that, in all probability, no genius could paint the whole picture.

The young woman broke down with the sobbing of a wronged child. She stammered out that her world was in collapse around her. The ideology of National Socialism, in which she had believed so enthusiastically, was a nightmarish fraud. Now she was surrounded by a shattering void.

I could not feel sorry for her.

TEN

Most of the people were still asleep on the floor of the gym when I left. As I made toward the center of the city, I faced the destruction of whole blocks in ruins. Here and there people were rummaging in the ruins, aimlessly trying to recover things.

This was Nuremberg, the Mecca of the National Socialist Party. Here was a picture of the destruction Germany brought down on Europe and itself. Not so long ago these streets had resounded with Hitler's frenzied speeches, and jubilant German masses gathered from all over the country to sanction everything their Party stood for. In their arrogance, they were going to build their 1,000 year empire on the ruins of all Europe. The Nazis' devastating punishment was in front of my eyes. I felt no joy at the destruction of the deadliest enemy human kind had ever encountered. Neither did I experience any sorrow. It was like walking through a cemetery with no emotional ties to it. My own losses were apparently too great for me to feel anything else.

Considering that it was early in the morning, the streets were crowded. American military vehicles zoomed in every direction. Many civilian trucks also moved through the streets, repeatedly stopping for crowds demanding a lift out of the city. Most of them were women with backpacks on their shoulders going to the countryside in search of food to be traded for the wares they were carrying.

I managed to get on a truck headed for Regensburg. On the bumpy ride, I listened to people talking about trading with farmers for food. Their other popular subject were the Amis, the Americans, whom they derided as silly young boys with no culture whatsoever. Their preoccupation with throwing and catching a small ball, and constantly chewing gum was ridiculed. To me, this kind of talk was just another aspect of German arrogance. They had the nerve to consider themselves civilized, despite their barbaric wartime misbehavior. Hopefully all the concentration camps with their gas chambers and crematoriums would be made into monuments, to remind the world not to trust Germans with power. I despised them for their Teutonic "superior culture."

After stops in many villages to let people out, we arrived in Regensburg. The fact that it was the ancient Ratisbona with pre-Roman roots tempted me to stop. But I was anxious to move on, impatient that there might be an important message waiting for me in the Jewish Information Office.

Luckily, I got a lift to Landshut on a truck. We arrived early in the afternoon at the outskirts of town. I sat at the side of the road, under a tree near a brooklet. I was hungry, not having eaten since early morning. In my knapsack, I still had some of the bread and cheese that Sofia had provided for my journey. I ate, relishing every bite. The water from the brook was cold and refreshing. I stretched out on the grass, put the knapsack under my head, and closed my eyes.

Landshut. It was through Landshut that we had been dragging ourselves on the fifth day of the death march. There had remained only a small group of us, surviving on only the energy of sheer willpower not to succumb. I remembered a little house near the street, and the old woman in the front yard filling a pail with water from a hand pump. It must had been the flow of the water that had driven insane our column of miserables who appeared on the street. We had broken ranks and rushed to the pump, begging for water. The guards had been right on top of us, smashing us with their rifles and shouting obscenities. Then a few shots had rung out. Several corpses had been left in the front yard, and the column of desperately thirsty condemned souls had moved again down the road. At the pump, the old woman kept calling out to the guards, *"Seit ihr verrickt worden? Seit ihr alle verrickt worden?* Have you gone crazy? Have you all gone crazy?"

Back on the road and back in control, the guards near me had started to talk about the new wonder arms that the Fuehrer had been promising. They would destroy the enemy and secure victory for Germany. The guards had sounded absolutely confident. And I? I could not get depressed. I was beyond the ability to react, just a walking automaton.

Now, by the roadside I regretted that there was no way to locate the old lady with the hand pump in the front yard. I got on the road and started walking toward the center of the city. Two Americans in a jeep pulled over and asked for my identification papers. My uniform had drawn their attention. One of them spoke broken German in which it was easy for me to detect a rich mixture of Yiddish words. I quickly made him understand that I was Jewish. When they learned that I was going to Dachau, they offered me a lift. They were going to Schleisheim, the Munich suburb which was on the way.

The ranking officer said something to the driver, and moved to the back seat next to me. He introduced himself as Capt. Jacob R. We didn't stop talking. He wanted to know everything about me, and was visibly moved by my story. When I told him about the Jewish Information Office in Dachau, he became very interested in our work. He was attached to a unit of the occupation army which had the task of searching out and arresting prominent Nazis. It might be important for him to pay an official visit to my office, he said.

We got so involved in our conversation that our arrival in Schleisheim caught us by surprise. Capt. Jacob told the driver, whom he called Pat, to take me to Dachau. Before I left, he filled my knapsack with cigarettes, chocolate, and coffee. Our parting was very warm, and he assured me once more that he would see me in Dachau.

Within a half hour, Pat let me off in front of the gate to the Dachau camp. I found out that in my absence, the J.I.O. had finally been assigned a small building in the former SS administration area. The American authorities needed the former concentration camp to house the imprisoned SS men and other important Nazis. The fenced-in camp had to be cleared quickly.

My welcome back was warm. My friend Yosef had reserved for me the other bed in the room he occupied.

The two-story house was small. On the ground floor the entrance hall led to a large room, which had become the office of the J.I.O. It was furnished with a number of desks, filing cabinets, and three typewriters. At the end of the entrance hall was a kitchen, a store room, and the common bath and toilet facilities. The stairs to the upper floor led to a balcony which faced the main door, and overlooked the entrance hall. Off the balcony were four doors to rooms which served as bedrooms. Each was shared by two or more persons.

During my absence, significant changes had occurred in our organization. Mietek had secured for himself the position of Administrator of the Dachau prison, where the American authorities were now keeping Nazi officials of special importance. Among them was the SS woman, Ilse Koch. She was infamously known for picking out prisoners with attractive tattoos, and having them killed. From their skins, she made lampshades and purses. It was at first thought that she faced a certain death sentence. But there was a rumor that a man had been allowed to enter her cell and impregnate her, to prevent the death sentence. I asked Mietek to resign from the J.I.O. and he complied.

Only three of us original founders of the J.I.O. remained, Yosef Lindenberg, Yakob Zylberstein, and I. While I was away, Yakob had learned that his wife's younger sister had survived and was in Kaunitz near Lipstadt. His wife with her little girl had perished in the Auschwitz gas chamber when their transport train arrived from Radom. Yakob had gone immediately to Kaunitz, and brought the young woman with him to Dachau. They had agreed to start a new life together, and occupied one of the rooms.

Another room was occupied by Yakob's three sisters, who had survived Auschwitz and other concentration camps. They had learned of their brother's whereabouts and had come to join him.

The third room was used by three people who had attached themselves to us. They were Marian W. with his teenage sons, Arno and Wladek C. All three survived death camps.

With his new wife and sisters to take care of, Yakob needed income. An American officer helped him get the position of trustee in a local factory which was under surveillance. This left only Yosef and me to run the J.I.O. By mutual agreement, I was the president and he was the secretary.

Determined to travel to Poland to search for surviving relatives, I registered with the Polish Committee to be included in the next transport of repatriates. But Yosef said it would be a wrong move. He argued that the Dachau J.I.O. now was quite well known among survivors in Germany and had become our established address. If there were any survivors in our families, they were bound to hear about us. I cancelled the trip to Poland. Yosef and I continued with the work of the J.I.O.

Following the broadcast of our first list of the Jewish survivors in Dachau on Swiss radio, while I was away the first volume of the *Sharit Ha-Platah,* the *Book of the Living,* got into print through the help of Rabbi Abraham J. Klausner, Chaplain, U.S. Army.

On page six were the names of those of us who had formed the J.I.O. after our liberation. There was, however, no mention of our organization. Nor was, to our surprise, any credit given for our initiative in starting the registration of Dachau survivors and deceased. We were very proud of our accomplishments. Someone said, we certainly deserved as much recognition as the three unknown-to-us Americans to whom the book had been dedicated. We felt slighted by the omission. We assumed it had not been done intentionally, and decided not to tell the Rabbi about our hurt feelings.

The Foreword was signed, "Abraham J. Klausner, Chaplain, U.S.A., Dachau, Concentration Camp, June 26, 1945." This was followed in English and German by seven Articles on the Status of Jews.

Regarding the Status:

1. No Jew need to return to his native land.
2. Those desiring to return will be transported at such time as the regular transports to that country are in progress.
3. Immigration problems will be handled on an individual basis by the Joint Distribution Committee.
4. This means is only one of a series through which families can be contacted. It is possible at present to contact friends and relatives living in the Americas, England, France, Switzerland, Palestine and Africa. In the case of United States of America, the complete address is not essential. The name and state will suffice. Each camp leader is aware of the procedure.
5. Until such time when the Jew will once again be free to live and build as he chooses, we shall endeavor to serve his every need. Schools are established in the larger camps, and the religious needs of all are being supplied. The great libraries of Warsaw, stolen by the Nazis, have been recovered, and the volumes are being distributed to all camps. We ask that you make known to us every problem so that we can adequately serve you.
6. Should you find a name in these lists and want to contact the individual, note the fact to your camp committee. Arrangements, wherever possible, will be made for such a meeting.
7. Check lists for your own name. If it does not appear, request your leader to present your name for printing in the next volume.

The first volume of *Sharit Ha-Platah* contained the names of Jewish survivors in twelve camps in Bavaria, Dachau, Freiman, Landsberg, Schleisheim, Pensing, St. Ottelia, Neustift, Feldafing, Passing, Buchberg, Mittenwald, and Garmisch.

When I returned from my trip, work on the second volume was in progress. More emphasis was being put on grouping the names in different camps by nationalities, and in alphabetical order.

The second volume of *Sharit Ha-Platah*, Bavaria, Buchenwald and others was dated Dachau, Concentration Camp, July 20, 1945, and dedicated to two unknown-to-us lieutenants.

ELEVEN

It was the end of July. Three months had passed since that unbelievable afternoon in April when the Americans had entered the Dachau Concentration Camp and freed about 33,000 condemned men from all the lands of Europe, among them about 2,000 Jews of different nationalities. On May 8, the war in Europe had ended with the unconditional surrender of Germany.

We, the former prisoners of the concentration camps, were now called inmates of a particular camp, or just D.P.'s, Displaced Persons. During the past three months, many had been repatriated. Many others, however, including all the Jews from Eastern Europe had remained in West Germany. Almost all of them lived in D.P. camps which had been put under the administration of UNRRA, the United Nations Relief and Rehabilitation Organization. Most of these camps were surrounded by barbed wire fences, and guarded by American military personnel. A pass was needed to leave and enter the camps.

The D.P.'s had no choice of a place to live since the camps were the only places where they could get lodging and food. A quantity of two-tier bunks to a room resulting in crowded living conditions. The monotonous diet of 2,000 calories a day included soup, black bread, sausage, and cheese. Such conditions did not generate a cheerful outlook for the future. With the good things of liberation taken into account, the sad fact remained that the survivors continued to live in crowded and regimented camps.

Some managed to get employment with the American military, and secured private lodgings. Through their contacts, they obtained American goods like cigarettes, chocolate, coffee, and chewing gum, which were very much in demand by the German population and had enormous trading value.

The Jewish survivors of Dachau who were recovering from malnutrition or had tuberculosis, had been transferred to the hospital of St. Ottilien for general illnesses, or to Gauting for tuberculosis.

Some Jews had joined relatives or friends at D.P. camps in Feldafing, Landsberg and Schleisheim. Those three camps accounted for the majority of the Jewish D.P. population in Bavaria, an estimated 14,000 men, women, and a small number of children. Some of the young men who were in good physical condition disappeared. It was no secret that they had joined the *Bricha*, the Jewish Brigade in Palestine.

The *Bricha* became very active in Europe. This dedicated organization of patriotic Palestinian Jews was smuggling survivors from the countries of Eastern Europe to bring them to Palestine. It devoted a special effort to rescue Jewish children who survived in Christian homes. Most of those children were raised as Catholics and their rescuers resisted giving them up.

In June 1945, delegates from different camps gathered in Feldafing, and formed the Central Committee of Liberated Jews in Bavaria. Its first priority was to determine the needs of the homeless Jews. The Allied authorities were very slow to organize any relief activities. There was practically no supply of food, drugs, or clothing.

Dr. Zalman Grinberg, a survivor from Lithuania, was elected President of the Central Committee. Its offices were established at the Deutsches Museum in Munich.

As officials of the Jewish Information Office in Dachau, we became employees of the Central Committee. In the next few months it began to be funded and we started to draw small salaries in German marks.

Sometime in June, we started to receive food parcels. This helped to improve our drab diet.

From time to time, the camp administration had been giving us an allotment of wares from the former SS warehouses. These included dark brown cakes of soap that were very rich in caustic soda, textiles for military uniforms, fur-lined winter army boots, and other items which the SS had been hoarding behind the front lines. Usually we could trade these items for things we most desired, like fruit, vegetables and civilian clothing.

Of all the things our American friends introduced us to, the most appreciated was white DDT power. Our bedding and clothing were heavily and frequently sprayed. The guards were provided with spray guns filled with DDT. Every time we passed through, they gave us full blasts behind the collar in front and back, and then down into our trousers. It did not matter if we had passed the post only minutes before. The procedure was repeated. What mattered was that the dreadful lice disappeared. For this we were very grateful.

Happily we had almost no contact with the German population, since we were under the jurisdiction of the American Headquarters of the Dachau camp compound. The Americans and their customs were an enigma. Their informality was far beyond that in our prewar lives. It was hard for us to see men, including officers of high rank, sitting with their feet on top of their desks, and staying that way when someone came to see them. The constant chewing of gum, even during conversation, was very strange to us. Men in the office would freely ask one another how to spell certain words. Our background was that a person of gymnasium, high school education, had to know how to spell well. We would have been embarrassed to admit otherwise. It was also very strange to us that in shaking hands, many men omitted doing so with women. It seemed to be an accepted custom, because the women nodded their heads with a smile.

The enthusiasm for the game of baseball was another thing we talked about among ourselves. We marveled at the persistence of the young soldiers, throwing and catching a little ball for long stretches while chewing gum. Only when they were playing an actual game, with soldiers and officers screaming out the score, could we identify with their enthusiasm. We behaved that way at our soccer games.

Generally our relationship was friendly. Many people developed personal relationships. It was the language barrier that stood in our way. We did not speak English, and very few Americans knew any other language than their own. Communication was better with descendants of European immigrants who had learned their parents' tongues. Most often this involved American Jews. They usually had a little knowledge of Yiddish, German, Polish, Russian, Ukrainian or one of the Balkan languages. They also took the most initiative toward helping us learn the fate of relatives who had stayed in the countries from which we D.P.'s had emigrated. Through them, some of us also tried to establish contact with relatives in the U.S.A.

By now the only nationality still in Dachau in significant number was the Polish group. It consisted of individuals who, for their own reasons, had refused to return to Poland. We of the Jewish Information Office, being mostly of Polish origin, kept a neighborly relationship with the Poles, especially with the committee members. The basis of the relationship was mutual cooperation in pursuing the common interests of our D.P. status. They held the former concentration camp's documents which they had taken over from the former International Committee. To get information that pertained to the Jews, we regularly spent time in the Polish Office.

Since early June, the registration of the living Jewish survivors had become a simple matter. Most of the very sick had died during the first weeks of May. Those who lingered on had been transferred to the hospitals in St. Ottelien, Gauting, and Amberg.

We also maintained a vigil over the graves in the common cemetery for former prisoners of all faiths from the Dachau

Concentration Camp established after the liberation, to bury the huge numbers of corpses piled up in and around the camp, and the remains of those who had died during the weeks after liberation.

A mass grave of prisoners had been discovered in the nearby place called Prittelbach, some weeks after the camp was liberated. At the time, it was estimated that it contained the bodies of 12,000 murdered prisoners. A Cross and a Star of David had been erected on tall posts by the survivors near each other on top on that grave. We were dismayed to discover a short time later that the post with the Star of David had been overturned. We repaired the damage, and then kept a constant vigil over the place. The vandals were never found.

For a while, the count of the Jews registered in our office remained rather constant. We turned our attention to the meticulously kept total lists of the deceased in the former concentration camp. We decided to extract from them the names of the Jewish victims. To our surprise, those lists included not only names in branches belonging to Dachau, but also people from many other camps. We discovered that those were the camps to which the prisoners had been deported from Dachau. We decided to add to those lists the names registered by us of those who had died after the liberation. Yosef took on this job, and gave his full attention to it.

Two years later I took those lists of about 25,000 Jewish victims' names to the United States. They were published by the Jewish Labor Committee in New York under the title "*Yorzait*, Memorial Dates." Wherever possible, next to the first and last names appeared the date and place of birth, and the date of death.

Volume 1 contained names of Jews born in Lithuania, Latvia, Estonia, and White Russia. Volume 2 listed Jews born in Poland. Later these books were recognized as legal documents for proving the death of a person whose name appeared in them.

By the end of July 1945, a new problem arose. It involved
the D.P.'s and the camp M.P.'s, the occupational authorities'
military police. Some D.P.'s got involved in the black
market, mainly with American cigarettes, chocolate, chewing gum, and some other items. The G.I.'s purchased those
items in the P.X. military stores at special low prices. They
paid for them with Military Payment Certificates which had
the value of the American dollar, but could be used only in
the occupied zone. Americans could exchange the certificates for real dollars when they were leaving for the United
States.

A three-way market developed involving some American
personnel, the German population and the D.P.'s. The
Americans sold the wares to the D.P.'s at marked-up prices,
for certificates or valuables like cameras or jewelry. The
D.P.'s sold the wares to the Germans, either for German
marks or in exchange for many kinds of valuables. Conse-
quently, a black market developed in dollars, certificates,
and German marks as means of payment.

The M.P.'s got an order to end the black market. The
problem developed when they pursued the D.P.'s as if they
were the only culprits. We presented the easiest target, because most of us lived in guarded camps. It was easy for the
M.P.'s to stage unexpected raids in the camps and ap-
prehend those with whom they found the wares. Usually the
wares and money were confiscated on the spot, and the accused was not given a chance to clear himself and claim his
property. Most of the time, he was then set free. By target-
ing only D.P.'s and not Germans or Americans, the M.P.'s did
not close down the black market.

Many of our American friends were indignant about the
situation. They wished to expose the Germans and the
Americans who were out to enrich themselves. They also
could see our point, that for the survivors involved, those
transactions were their only immediate chance to improve
their living conditions.

Through this and other encounters, it was becoming obvious that some authorities considered us a nuisance, and an impediment to the smooth administration of the Occupied Zone. This attitude came from the highest levels of the administration. Some of our friends promised to write their members of Congress about the sorry living conditions of the D.P.'s in the Occupied Zone.

TWELVE

It was early on the sunny afternoon of the last day of July 1945. I was leaving my room to return to the office downstairs, when I heard a commotion in the entrance hall. From the balcony, I looked down on an unbelievable scene. There was Wladek, with the almost square body frame of a bear, topped by a moon face and a shiny bald head, his arms wrapped tightly around a most beautiful young woman. Her face radiated, and her happy laughter resounded in the hall. Her blonde hair was delightfully in disarray around her beaming face. Her laughter reminded me of joyous bells, against the background of Wladek's bellowing while he whirled her around.

Another young girl watched the scene timidly but with a happy smile. From the balcony, I clearly was seeing a happy reunion. As if feeling my eyes on her, the lovely blonde girl looked up. Our eyes met, and we both smiled in a silent greeting. Wladek did the introductions. The young blonde beauty was Gina Rachman, the daughter of Wladek's former acquaintance in a Warsaw printing business. They had been together in a number of camps after they had been deported from the Warsaw ghetto. Since the deportation around August 1944, from the forced labor camp in Radom, they had lost sight of each other.

Gina introduced her quiet companion, Nunia M., the younger sister of her friend Mania. Both had survived Bergen-Belsen, where they had been deported from Auschwitz. The two were visibly exhausted from their trip. We showed them to our guest room.

Wladek could not stop talking about Gina. Still a kid at

the time of the ghetto, she had been known by her diminutive name, Ginka.

Wladek and Ginka's father had been together in print shops of the Small Warsaw Ghetto until its liquidation in May 1943, when the Germans declared Warsaw *Judenrein*, free of Jews. About 100 printers had been forced into cattle cars bound for an unknown destination. After the hot, suffocating transport in crammed box cars, they had finally been unloaded into the hell of the Poniatow-Maidanek death camps. Then, suddenly, the members of the printer's group had been collected by the SS a month later, and had been shipped to the forced labor camp at Radom.

Almost daily, we had been receiving a flow of visitors from all over West Germany. They had heard about our Jewish Information Office, and came hoping to find out something about a husband, wife, daughter, son, parents, or friends. Usually it was the sadness of not having information, or of confirming that the people had not survived. On very rare occasions, a visitor came from the home city of someone in our group. Most often we exchanged questions and information about the many unaccounted for.

The sudden visit of the two girls brought great excitement. The girls also knew Yakob, his new wife, and his three sisters. They and Nunia had all grown up in Radom, and had known each other since childhood. Gina was a child of the printers' group from Warsaw.

Late in the afternoon, the two girls came down for the evening meal in the cafeteria. They looked refreshed. Nunia, a Jewish teenager in Dachau, was to all of us a sentimental link with our past. Gina commanded everyone's attention. She was sheer beauty, a delight to look at.

Gina was a phenomenon. Her features were not those of a classic beauty. She had a slightly prominent nose with a little arc. Its shape fit her face perfectly. She had a slightly curled chin and a high forehead. Her big brown eyes were full of sparkles, of lively shimmers. The ends of her eye brows slanted upward, as if she was wondering about something. The golden blonde hair was a lovely curtain around the stage of her face.

Something else also drew people to her, her wit, and the kindness she showed toward everybody.

Gina wore the short sleeved white dress in which she had arrived. On her left forearm was the tattooed number from Auschwitz. The numbers were small and unusually neat. I could make them out when I went over to greet her. "A24639."

It was hard to believe that this radiant young woman survived the Warsaw ghetto, from its start when she was a young teenager, to its liquidation, and on top of that, the death camps of Poniatow, Maidanek, and Auschwitz. What quality did it take, I wondered, to emerge miraculously from all those gehennas, and spring back to her vibrant spirit and radiating girlish attractiveness?

In the cafeteria, we arranged a few tables into a close group. There was a lot of kidding and laughter. The Polish group kept their eyes on us. Gina, we learned, had come to Dachau looking for information about her younger brother. Nunia was looking for her father. They had heard that Wladek had been with the two men in the Vaihingen Concentration Camp. On their dangerous journey, they had hitch-hiked on military trucks, in freight railroad cars, and by any other means they could find. Unfortunately, Wladek told them, he had been moved to Dachau, and did not know the fate of those who had remained in Vaihingen.

We returned to our place for coffee and more talk. We wanted to hear more about the lots of our guests, after they had been chosen by Dr. Mengele at Auschwitz for slave work in German war industry.

We pushed a few tables together in the office, and gathered chairs around them. Soon the table held a large steaming pot of coffee and a generous supply of cigarettes. Gina first asked Wladek and Yakob what had happened to the men after the SS separated them from the women and children. The two men told the story of the few remaining Radom Jews.

By the end of July 1944, exactly one year before, the Germans had surrounded the Jews of Radom and terrorized them into forming a marching column. That had been the beginning of the murderous march to the city of Tomaszow where they had finally arrived after four or five days. There the SS guards had separated the men from the women and the children, and it was there that Yakob had seen his wife and his little daughter for the last time. That much Gina and Nunia had known because both had been in that march. What had happened after that, they were eager to know.

The SS men had loaded the Jewish men into cattle cars. The train then had headed for Auschwitz. Only after the liberation had those who survived found out that their women and children had been on the same train, in cattle cars behind them.

Arriving at Auschwitz, the men had been evacuated from the cars, terrorized by beatings and shouting. An on-the-spot selection had taken place. The old and sick had been loaded onto trucks, destination gas chamber. The rest had been forced back into the cattle cars. After many days of suffering, the train had arrived in Vaihingen, a hell-like concentration camp close to Stuttgart.

Vaihingen had been established on a swamp. The ground of the camp was covered with mud for most of the year. Lack of sanitary conditions and miserable food rations that did not satisfy nagging hunger, had been responsible for a very high death rate among the inmates. Mass graves had been in use. Late in the fall of 1944, the Germans had started to evacuate Vaihingen. Inmates who could still walk had formed into columns, and had been marched toward Dachau at various time intervals. Others had been put on rail transports. Very many had perished in those transports.

Some inmates had remained in Vaihingen, and had been liberated by the advancing French army. We heard that the French had been shocked by the horrors of Vaihingen, the first concentration camp they had seen. They had moved the sick to local hospitals, and the others to a nearby village which the German population had been forced to evacuate, leaving everything behind. There were rumors that among the liberated had been about 200 men from Radom.

Neither Wladek nor Yakob knew anything about the fate of Nunia's father nor Gina's teenage brother, Sevek. For a long time, the smoke-filled room was silent. We all felt heartbroken for our guests.

It was late. Only Gina, Yosef, and I remained in the room chain smoking cigarettes in silence. After a while, I asked Gina if she would tell us the story of the printer's group. Finally, lighting a new cigarette, she said with a faint smile that it might be better than retiring for the night and being alone with her thoughts.

Gina had had a happy childhood in her parents' affluent household. Her father had left Russia after the revolution and had established a highly successful business in Warsaw's printing world.

After the Germans occupied Warsaw, they had consolidated all printing plants, including his, under one management. The German in charge, realizing the management abilities of Yono Rachman, Gina's father, had appointed him manager. Because the Jewish printers pampered and bribed the German, he had started to protect the group, and had even listed many wives and some children as expert printers. Included had been Gina, her mother, and her brother. The plant was located in the small ghetto, where the printers and their families had found a relatively peaceful existence.

Yono Rachman had looked ahead and had come up with a scheme. The year 1943 continued with bad reverses for the Germans. The Russians had reached the former eastern border of Poland. Yono Rachman had proposed to the German a plan for keeping his position and avoiding being sent to the front.

The proposal was that the German convince his superiors of the importance of preserving the printing plant for the war effort, and that he get their permission to move it to the west. His experienced Jewish workers would go along so that the equipment could be reassembled and put into operation in the new location with minimum loss of time.

The German had been spoiled by the special cooking done for him by the Jewish women, and by the many gifts he had been receiving. One day, he informed Rachman that he had gotten the permission for the plan.

The group had survived the April 1943 ghetto uprising. Early in May, the final liquidation of the Warsaw ghetto had been ordered, and the Jews had been marched to the Umschlagplatz to the cheers of the Polish population. Yono Rachman and a few other men had been left to dismantle and crate the printing presses. The group was told that their names, as specialized workers, had been submitted to the authorities. They were to be sent to the new location of the printing plant.

At the Umschlagplatz, the printers and their families had been crammed into box cars. The heat was unbearable. People had begged for water. Gina had been together with her mother and brother. Through a hole in the car, she had begged the Ukrainian watchman for water, offering her mother's diamond ring in exchange. He had demanded the ring in advance. She had given it to him, hardly expecting that he would keep his side of the bargain. To her surprise, he had come back with a small container of water. No sooner had she gotten it than people around her had grabbed it and spilled the precious bit of water.

After torturous days of travel, the Jews had been unloaded in death camps at Flugplatz, Poniatow, Lublin, and Maidanek. Gina and her brother had been kept in Flugplatz. Her mother had been taken to Maidanek, and her boyfriend to Poniatow. Gina said she did not wish to torture us with the description of those hell-places.

The conditions had been so monstrous that no one could expect to survive for long. Then a miracle. One day in June, the magic list of printer specialists had appeared. Printers and families from the various camps had been shipped by train to the city of Radom, western Poland, where a forced labor camp still existed. Gina's boyfriend and his family had not survived Poniatow.

When they had arrived in Radom, Gina had run along the platform crying "Where is my mother? Did anybody see my mother?" A friend from the printers' group had pointed to a shriveled old woman. Only a few weeks had passed, and she had not recognized her own mother who was only 40 years old.

The Jews from Radom had looked at the arriving group of about 100 people with bewilderment. The Radom Jews had lived through pogroms, resettlements, and ghetto confinement, but the new arrivals were a sorrowful picture of people obviously the victims of immense suffering. This was June 1944. The Radom ghetto survivors still had had no idea about conditions in the concentration and death camps.

As Gina, her mother, and her brother stood on the platform crying and hugging each other, a young woman went to them and invited them for the evening meal. She was Mania M. She took them to the one room which she shared with her husband. She arranged for them to take a bath, and replaced their lice-ridden rags. She obviously gave up some of her last possessions to get food for the meal.

Gina recalled the unforgettable impressions of the white tablecloth, the china plates and dinnerware, and the dignity of the meal. After dinner, Mania provided a place on the floor of her one-room apartment, so that Mrs. Rachman could spend the night with her children. That had been the beginning of the friendship between Gina and Mania M.

THIRTEEN

Next morning at breakfast in the Dachau cafeteria, our guests inquired about Dachau's size, and its capacity for gassing and cremating people. I volunteered to show them the concentration camp.

At the guardhouse, we submitted to the treatment of DDT. The two young G.I.'s must have considered the encounter with us something to break their boredom. With smiles on their faces, they both stepped out of the guardhouse armed with air pumps. They administered blasts of the white powder behind the collars of the girl's garments. Then they pointed to their chests. The girls facilitated a shot of DDT into their bosoms by opening a button or two of their dresses. I was embarrassed when the G.I. blasted the DDT into my trousers.

As we walked, Nunia remarked that the DDT experience was nothing compared with what had happened in former days. Then, new arrivals had had to stand naked in line, and submit to the shaving of the intimate parts of their bodies, usually by male inmates.

I felt that the remark was meant to ease my embarrassment over the DDT treatment. Gina mused that remarkably, in the short time since liberation, the sensitivities of a civilized society had taken ahold again. As a matter of fact, now we were even more sensitive to any act of humiliation or embarrassment. This somehow was especially true when it came from our liberators.

The size of the Dachau installation made it like a laboratory, compared to the gigantic operation of Auschwitz and Lublin, the girls said. The gaudy crematorium murals of colorful youngsters riding bare-back on frolicking pigs, and the inscriptions requiring cleanliness in that place, were further proof of German perversity. The mound of human ashes with fragments of charred bones reopened old wounds.

On the way to and from the crematorium, we looked at the German prisoners inside the wire fence, in the former concentration camp. I remarked that what we saw looked more like a recreation place than a prisoner camp. The Germans, most of them in uniforms, were sitting leisurely in the sun, and were involved in conversation, card games, or sport competitions. The towers with no guards looked abandoned.

At the guardpost, the same two G.I.'s waited for us with their air pumps at ready. In broken German they explained that they had to spray us again. Fortunately, both girls submitted with a sense of humor to the two eager soldiers performing their duty.

Just before we reached our house, Gina started to limp. Her shoes were in very bad disrepair. She had just lost the heel of one shoe. The soles on both were worn all the way through.

One of our people, an excellent shoemaker, was presently employed by the Americans. He was a big, good-natured fellow with a large KL tattoo on the upper side of his left wrist. He put his arm close to Gina's left forearm, on which was tattooed her Auschwitz number. Their smiles expressed the sadness of two persecuted victims. Our friend took the measurements of her feet, and with a gentle smile promised to have the shoes ready for her in a day, even if he had to work on them at night.

Taking the afternoon off, I sat with Gina in the shade of the big oak tree not far from the house. I asked her if she would continue with her story from the printers' arrival in Radom.

The printers' group, she said, had somehow found places in the overcrowded environment of the Radom forced labor camp. The printing presses had arrived within a week, and their installation quickly began. However, a few printers, including Gina's father, had not arrived from Warsaw. Soon the news had reached Radom, through the underground, that the men had been executed by the Germans the day they had finished crating the presses. It was a terrible blow for the Rachman family and for the printers who lost their leader.

The tough conditions of life in the labor camp and the struggle for survival had not allowed time for grieving. At nighttime, the painful tragedy kept emerging. Not only had Gina lost her father, but, as she had learned from people in the group, her boyfriend and his whole family had been killed in Poniatow. She had lost the two most important men in her life.

In the camp. Gina had to help her mother and brother to retain their jobs in the print shop and to preserve their status of seemingly valuable workers. Because the lives of the printers had been saved from the Lublin extermination camp in an unprecedented case, the other Radom inmates were convinced that belonging to that group offered safety. Influential individuals, by bribing the Germans, had gotten themselves assigned to work with the printers. To make room for them, the weak and defenseless individuals in the camp had been assigned to menial labor.

There was a great need to supplement the starvation rations in the camp. The Jews had been doing it by trading their last possessions with the Polish people, who would come to the camp fence and barter food for bargains. Some people in the camp had asked Gina to bargain for them, giving her garments to trade on their behalf. Then they would give her some of the food she had obtained in the deal. This helped to relieve the continuous hunger pains of her teenage brother, Sevek, who had suffered most. Often she or her mother pretended that they could not eat, and shared their food with him. His hunger as a growing boy seemed insatiable.

Gina stopped talking for a while. Then she looked at me with a sparkle in her eyes, and said that she would tell me something, but only if I would not make fun of her. I promised.

Late one afternoon, she explained, she had struck a deal with a young Polish fellow. He had given her, in addition to the agreed food, a quantity of tomatoes, a gift, he said. The problem was that the tomatoes were green, so there was little hope of trading them for bread. Somebody told Gina that tomatoes ripen in warm temperature and in darkness. She carried the tomatoes with her for the next few days, and kept them under her covers at night. At last they started to become pink, and then finally, red.

In the crowded camp, the tomatoes could not be kept a secret. Gina was kidded as the girl who slept with tomatoes. Since she had been rejecting the advances of men, the kidding had taken on a jeering camp humor flavor. Had she enjoyed sleeping with the tomatoes? Because of my promise, I resisted an urge to kid her a bit.

In the gruesome living conditions of the ghettos and labor camps, rules of normal prewar life were often disregarded. People improvised their own ways to lessen their misery. Men and women often got together to enjoy each others' company. Single girls who were alone usually accepted offers of men to move in with them. In the prevailing jargon, they were known as "cousins."

Was I getting an indirect message that Gina had never been a "cousin"? The pleasant thought entered my mind as she continued her story.

The life in the Radom forced labor camp had been very tough. The Germans kept eliminating the remaining children, the old, and the sick. The only hope had come from the Russian and Western fronts. News usually came from somebody in the camp who, despite the death penalty for possessing a radio, had listened in secrecy. The slightest successes of the Allies and adversities of the Germans had been sources of renewed hopes for surviving the Germans.

In July 1944, the Germans liquidated the camp, and

marched all its inmates to Tomaszow. As Yacob told us the previous night, there the Germans had separated the men from the women and the children. There, she said trembling, she had seen her brother for the last time.

Again there was no time to grieve because that same night, the women and children were loaded into cars of a waiting train under beatings and abusive shouting of the Germans and their Ukrainian henchmen.

In Auschwitz, they were put through a live-or-die selection commanded by Dr. Mengele. Gina and her mother had been directed to the side of those who would remain alive at least temporarily. Young children and their mothers, and the weak and ill were taken away toward the gas chambers and the smoke-belching crematorium. The stench of burning human bodies had defied description.

The memory of the condemned, especially of the young mothers hugging their children, on their way to death, was an unforgettable nightmare. Among them were some young women with children whom she had befriended in Radom. They were gassed and burned that day because they had hidden their children. Had any nation ever in history been so cruel, Gina asked?

The ancient Egyptians, I told her, had been close to the Nazis when they waged a war of annihilation after their Pharaoh decreed that all newborn Jewish males must be put to death. But the abominable crime of exterminating the Jewish people, conceived and executed by the Germans during the 1930's into the 1940's, had no precedent in past history. Even the Catholic Church, which had been spreading pernicious hatred toward the Jewish people for 19 centuries, had probably not foreseen such horrifying results. The Crusades, the Inquisition, the pogroms, and all the other persecutions of the Jews in Christian lands had been inhumanly cruel and had been warnings of events to come. They had been encouraged, and very often initiated, by both religious and civil authorities. There is no doubt that they had been examples for the Germans.

Gina wondered why so many people in every European country had helped the Germans exterminate Jews, even though the Nazis persecuted them, too.

I, too, was deep in thought. For 1,900 years priests had been emissaries of the Vatican in all those lands. They had painted the Jews as representing the devil on earth, and had consigned Jews to eternal condemnation "for rejecting and crucifying Jesus." The Church had sanctified this persecution as a deserved divinely decreed punishment. Such teachings, I thought, violated the very premises on which Christianity had been founded. Yet priests had continued to spread them as the holy truth of their faith. They had spread hatred of Jews in every land and had poisoned their followers' souls and minds.

In past times the Jews had at least had the choice of saving their lives by being converted. Until its partition at the end of the 18th Century, Poland had conferred nobility on Jews who converted to Christianity.

But in the 20th Century, the German people, under the rule of the National Socialist Party, had as its mission the unconditional extermination of all Jewish people. German human and industrial resources had moved far toward completing that task.

Looking at the fiery ball of the falling sun on the horizon, I heard Gina's anxious whisper: How can there be any hope for us in a world so full of hatred? Before I had a chance to answer, we heard Yosef's voice reminding us in his kidding way that the cafeteria would not stay open until the two of us finished whatever we were doing.

Again that evening, we pulled together chairs and tables in our office, and asked our guests to continue their story.

Gina spoke first. It is impossible, she said, to describe the everlasting misery of Auschwitz. She spoke of the continuous flow of trains with cargoes of men, women, and children from all over Europe. The sight of selected victims on their way to the gas chambers was too monstrous to comprehend. The human smoke pouring from the chimneys of the crematoriums, and everywhere the horrible smell of burning flesh had made Auschwitz earth's own hell.

It was a while before Gina could start again. The surviving women from the Radom transport had been assigned to the same barrack, and had supported each other like sisters. In that barrack, she said, she had had her most moving birthday celebration ever. That evening, after returning to the barrack, she had been asked to climb to a top bunk. There she had found her mother and her closest friends. One had handed her a whole crispy clean cabbage leaf as a gift from all of them. Their eyes had gleamed with pride in getting it for her. They had insisted that she eat it all herself. Hugging and kissing her, they had wished that her next birthday be celebrated in freedom. Except for the cabbage leaf, it was all they could offer.

Imagine, she said through tears, that has come true. I'm going to celebrate my next birthday as a free person.

In November 1944, the women of Gina's barrack were divided into groups and loaded into cattle cars for an unknown journey. She was lucky to be with her mother, but had been separated from Mania and Nunia. After long days and nights in a crowded freight car, they had arrived at the Lipstadt Concentration Camp which supplied slave labor to Krupp's munitions factories.

Gina was assigned to a huge machine which produced munition shells. The moving parts of the machine, the fire, and the running water around her had scared her half to death, but she was forced to keep moving various levers without respite.

Starvation rations and long hours of hard work under the watchful eyes of harsh supervisors had worn many inmates out until they died. Replacement Jews were brought in from headquarters camps.

Lipstadt had been a slave labor camp in which there were also non-Jewish males. They were conscript laborers from the occupied countries. The technically skilled worked as foremen and overseers. They were closely watched, but enjoyed some privileges because they were valuable slaves. Unless they tried to run away or committed sabotage, they could expect to stay alive until the end of the war. Some of these non-Jews, especially the Italians and the French, had shown compassion for the condemned Jews, and had tried to ease their suffering whenever possible.

From time to time, Gina would find a piece of bread or cheese which one of the non-Jews had inconspicuously left for her. Some of them had whispered, in broken German, words encouraging her not to give up, because the Allies were not far away and salvation was near. Words like this made it easier to live a day at a time.

In February they started to hear the night booms of distant artillery. The inmates had smiled inwardly, not daring to antagonize their oppressors.

In March, the sounds of war got closer and louder. The German guards and camp administrators had begun to get nervous. On one of the last days of March, they had announced the evacuation of the camp, and had divided the inmates into several groups. They marched the inmates out of the camp under the guard of middle-aged German reserve soldiers armed with rifles.

Gina's group had consisted of about 700 worn-out women who dragged their feet in the slow march. Even rifle shots and cursing of the guards could not speed up the column's pace.

One day during the dreadful march, Gina continued, the column had entered a narrow road between fields full of unharvested turnips. Her body had been hurting from hunger because they had not eaten since the march began. Disregarding strict orders under the penalty of being shot, she ran into the field, picked up a few turnips, and got back unnoticed by the guards. Proudly she had displayed the loot in her gathered skirt, jesting that the end of the war must be imminent since she had gotten so much food.

Hardly had she spoken when they had heard the clatter of tanks and saw white linen sheets being waved by German guards. They were English tanks. The soldiers displayed unbelievable compassion for the haggard unwashed women in repulsive rags. They gave the women all their rations, and even let many of the dirty, smelly creatures hug and kiss them to pour out their gratitude.

Somebody said it was April First, but it was certainly not April Fools Day. It really had happened on the road by the turnip field.

FOURTEEN

In Dachau, for the past few weeks we had been searching for a place in town suitable for locating the Jewish Information Office. The camp administration wanted us to vacate the camp.

Fortunately we located a vacant building that had formerly been a restaurant. We liked the ground floor of the four-story building. Above it were private apartments. The house was only a few hundred yards from the railroad station, and was near a branch of the post office. We succeeded in having it requisitioned for us by the occupation authorities.

Proudly we ordered stationery with our new address and telephone number:

Jewish Information Office   Dachau, den . . . . . 194 . . .
      Dachau   Fruhlingstrasse 4.
                       Telefon 477.

The next morning Leon, the shoemaker, came over with the shoes for Gina in his hands. They were made of a beautiful light blue, soft leather, and fitted her feet perfectly. Leon's face shone happily when Gina thanked him and placed a kiss on his cheek.

Yosef suggested that she test the shoes by walking to town with us for a look at the progress of work in our future office. After receiving our usual doses of DDT, we walked out onto the wide road called the Nibelungen Strasse. The masters of the Third German Empire had named the street leading to the horror chambers of their concentration camp, after the epic legend about the origin of the German nation.

116

A few German workers were on the job site. They had removed the beer bar and other fixtures of the former restaurant, and had started to paint.

I selected the front room, off the main hall, for my office. Yosef picked the room he wanted as the secretary's office. Gina and Nunia were impressed with the idea of the Jewish Information Office being away from the camp. I was impatient to move out from the camp, and to establish an independent J.I.O.

We strolled through the town, through clean streets decorated with beds of flowers. Crossing the stream that flows through the town of Dachau, we climbed many steps up a steep hill to the center of town. This was the business section, full of stores and office buildings. We came upon a seventeenth century castle and parish church, but somehow we were not impressed.

The town gave the impression that it had been spared from damage or suffering during the six-year world war which had just ended. Dachau even seemed to have prospered from the war.

We hardly spoke on our walk back to the camp. Only when we again entered Nibelungen Street did Yosef remark that this prosperous community had been living off of the concentration camp since its creation in 1933.

That afternoon I sat with Gina again under the big oak tree. I was eager to hear what had happened after the surprise rescue by the English. The exhausted group of women, Gina said, was taken to the nearby village of Kaunitz which had been deserted. Afraid of retribution by the advancing Allies for camp cruelty, they all fled, leaving even their animals unattended.

The Jewish women had occupied the houses, and made themselves as comfortable as possible. The English moved on to the combat line, and an American unit took their place.

The Americans had shown themselves to be wonderful young men, Gina said. They could not do enough to help the liberated women recover from their ordeals. One young G.I. was of Polish descent. When he had heard Gina speaking Polish, his face had lit up. He would bring the world to her feet, he said. Almost every day, he had appeared with gifts of G.I.'s rations, also linen, clothing, and food that he had obviously taken from the Germans. One special day, Gina heard his call from the yard. There he stood proudly displaying a real live cow. Now she would have a regular supply of fresh milk, he had said proudly. To his surprise, she was scared to go near the big animal.

One day the young soldier had to leave. His unit had been ordered to the front line. He hoped some day to take her to his parents' farm in Nebraska. She had not heard from him since.

After the arrival of the Jewish chaplain, Ben C., the women began to learn about survivors in other camps nearby, and about the stalag for Polish prisoners of war. To their surprise, there had been some Jewish officers. They came to Kaunitz as soon as they learned about the liberated Jewish women. One of them, a native of Warsaw, had found his daughter and had fainted on the spot.

One day the chaplain brought a list of survivors in Bergen-Belsen. Like everybody else, Gina and her mother pored hungrily over the pages, looking for familiar names. They found two, Mania and Nunia M., their friends from the Radom forced labor camp. They had heard about the hell of Bergen-Belsen. Gina decided that she had to get the two sisters out of there, no matter what it took.

She persuaded Chaplain Ben to take her to Bergen-Belsen in his army jeep. The chaplain's uniform magically overcame obstacles, and they quickly located the barrack where the two sisters were.

Gina wanted to go alone to meet her friends. Neither Mania nor Nunia were in the barrack, so she decided to wait for them. Their primitive bunk was like so many she had known in the camps. Yet, after liberation, the sisters still had to sleep in it.

Mania and Nunia arrived. They looked at the bunk and at Gina on it, bewildered and unable to utter a sound. Gina got up and called them idiots for not recognizing their old friend. They all broke down in tears and laughter, hugging and hugging.

Chaplain Ben had already arranged for the sisters to go with them. After arriving in Kaunitz, they had moved in with Gina and her mother. Then the wonderful chaplain, Ben C., got his orders to move on. She had not heard from him since, Gina said, her voice choking. Old friends and family were gone, and now she was losing new friends, Gina said through tears.

Kaunitz, an obscure peasant village, had become a most unusual community. More than 700 women of many nationalities, Polish and Hungarian predominating, made up a most unusual population. They had begun to recover physically and mentally from their traumatic war experiences. Most of them had been young women with enough physical and mental stamina to survive. Now they had begun to improve their living conditions bit by bit. With materials they had found in the houses, they made dresses, skirts, and blouses. In a few weeks, many had changed so much that they no longer looked like the recently liberated creatures of exhaustion and despair.

The American G.I.'s had had an enormous influence on the recovery and well-being of the women. Many G.I.'s were charming and witty. The young Americans had become attracted to the young women. Soon many romantic relationships had sprung up. Merrymaking had become the main goal in life for many of the women.

I told Gina about my meeting with Sofia and Ala, and asked her if she would get in touch with them since she was planning to go to Stuttgart. She promised to see them.

One evening while I was in the office, typing with one finger, I felt a presence in the room, and looked up. It was Gina. I was only too glad for the excuse to get away from the typewriter.

We lit cigarettes and talked about our visit in the town of Dachau. She tried out one of the typewriters. I suggested that each of us write separately on any subject that was going through our minds. She wanted a specific topic so we agreed on, "It all had gone like smoke from a cigarette."

We sat at the typewriters for a long time, but neither of us wrote anything. Finally, realizing that the topic brought back painful memories, we agreed to abandon the idea.

Gina asked my opinion if it was going to be possible for us to live among people who had displayed such awesome hatred toward us Jews during these years of mortal persecution. It took a while to begin. Then I told her about my friendship in Dachau with the two Polish Catholic priests, Anton and Lech, a story I thought might inspire belief in the basic goodness of man, whatever his origin and belief.

She listened like a child being told a fairy tale. When I told her of Lech's plans for preaching to the Polish people about early Christian beliefs, and the truth about their own sinful hatred toward the Jewish people, tears filled her eyes and she said sadly that they are going to kill him; will mortify him as the blasphemous Antichrist. How could he ever hope to convince them that what the Church had been preaching for almost 2,000 years was hatred based on lies? How could he be so naive? she asked.

I admitted that I was also very much concerned about my friend. At our parting, just before his repatriation, he had told me about the inspiration he had experienced on his last visit to the crematorium. He had been on his knees at the pile of human ashes, praying for the souls of those who had perished there. Suddenly it had dawned on him that all those responsible for the heinous crimes had been Christians. He thought of the immense burden of guilt the Church had to shoulder. The sin of blaming the Jews for a crime they had never committed had been awesome. The Church teaching, that the Jewish people were damned for all future generations seemed the most cruel doctrine ever conceived. At different times in history church leaders had initiated and sponsored persecutions of the Jewish people and of nonconformists whom they called "heretics." Still, Lech knelt by the pile of Jewish ashes.

Still, I had not answered Gina's question. I pointed out to her that our Jewish Information Office contained some of my answer to her question. After liberation, the Americans had refused us permission to organize a Jewish Committee the way the nationalities in the camp had done. We had not been nationals of a Jewish state, they had said.

The few of us who had proposed a Jewish Committee had persisted. We had been singled out, we insisted, from among the people of all those nations as Jews to be persecuted and eliminated by mass murder. Nobody had cared then about our nationalities. As survivors, we had decided to renounce our former nationalities, and to declare our Jewish Nationality. We were willing to be stateless until a Jewish homeland was created in Palestine. We began to describe our nationality as "former," as in "former Polish." This had become widely accepted.

No, I answered Gina, I did not believe that it would be possible for us to live in any of our "former" European countries again. They had been so hopelessly permeated with hatred toward us and I did not believe any authority was willing to set things straight.

Our problem was that we, the survivors, had been stuck in the miserable D.P. camps. We had to live in the midst of our former executioners who had been allowed to remain in their comfortable homes, living off blood-stained spoils all over Europe. So far, not even the U.S.A. had volunteered to permit D.P. immigration. A lot of haggling was going on about how to limit immigrants to a very small number.

It was terribly painful to hear that with cruel determination the English blocked all attempts of the survivors to get to Palestine. We had received sporadic news about the barbaric treatment the survivors of concentration camps had been receiving on high seas, and on the shores of their Promised Land. While this was happening, no country had volunteered to admit survivors. During the war years, all of them had looked with indifference at our demise.

After the war had ended, there was no compassion from governments, even after the cruelties of the German concentration camps had been revealed. Let's face it, I said with conviction, it is still a hostile world we have to face, even after Nazi Germany has been defeated.

"Here in Germany," I continued, "two slogans have been coined and spread as if by planned agreement. One was, 'Wir haben Ja nichts gewust. We certainly did not know anything.'"

The magnitude of the operations of the very many concentration camps all over Germany could not have gone unnoticed by anybody, I told Gina. Even here in Dachau, so close to the camp, the people unashamedly insisted that they had been unaware of anything. This showed that within the German population, there was only the drive to deny any guilt, and no sign of remorse.

The second slogan was, "The Nazis did it." Blame the Nazis for everything became the motto nationwide.

The word "Nazis" was substituted for "Germans" to assign the blame for all the atrocities and the murder of tens of millions of people in Europe to a proportionally small German organization. The truth of history is that the whole German population accepted and supported Hitler and his organization of thugs, with the greatest of enthusiasm. Probably some Germans had reservations, but nobody had heard them while Germany successfully conquered and cruelly subjugated one European country after another. The world should consider everyone of them guilty until proven otherwise.

In the meantime, the two-slogan strategy was working. The Americans and even some D.P.'s referred to "Nazis" instead of "Germans" when the subject of war crimes came up. There was an attempt to confine the guilt of the German people to the numerically small Nazi organization. This was just the opposite of what the Christian world had been doing throughout the centuries of persecuting the Jews. All Jews had been judged guilty, and had suffered death and disaster without having committed any wrong.

As I spoke, Gina had chain smoked one cigarette after another. I continued. The Germans don't like to talk about concentration camps, crematoria, and gas chambers. They try to erase them from memory. We should not be surprised if the ugly deeds of the Hitler era are eliminated from German history books. It would be left to us, the survivors, to tell what has transpired. And it would be very hard to make people believe that all those unimaginable crimes against humanity were really committed in the heart of Europe. Hopefully, the Allies would protect the death and slave camps, with all their paraphernalia, from being plowed under by the Germans.

It was far past midnight. On the way upstairs, I commented that during all the time we had spent in the office, nobody had joined us. Gina blushed.

The next day Gina and Nunia left for the railroad station on Fruehling Strasse in the village of Dachau, on their way to Stuttgart.

FIFTEEN

On August 8th, 1945, news reached us that the U.S.A. had dropped an atom bomb on Hiroshima, Japan. I listened to the details of the devastating power of this new weapon, and tried to comprehend it. Suddenly, the immense power concentrated in a single atom had become the power of destruction. Fortunately for us, it had happened so far away that it almost seemed unreal.

On August 10th, we heard that the second atom bomb had been dropped on Nagasaki. The shocking details of death and devastation were assuaged somewhat by the happiness of our American friends, who joyously celebrated the end of the war and the prospect of returning home. Now they would not be shipped to the Far Eastern front.

One morning in August, an American jeep halted in front of our building, and Capt. Jacob R. stepped into our office. We shook hands vigorously like old acquaintances despite the fact that our only previous encounter had been Landshut when he gave me a lift to Dachau. He informed me that on this day there would be a review of the SS men interned in the camp. He had arranged for various groups of former concentration camp inmates to be brought to Dachau in order to identify any of the SS prisoners with their past activities in many concentration camps. He invited me to join him and watch the proceeding.

Outside the camp, former inmates were standing three and four deep. All were intensely watching the German prisoners as they passed by slowly inside the fence under the supervision of American M.P.'s. A young woman standing next to an M.P. turned around, looked at me, and exclaimed, "Mr. Sack. Aren't you engineer Sack from Borys-law?"

I kept looking at the young woman, straining to recall who she could be. Then she said with a smile, "I am Sarah K., the daughter of the grocery man your wife used to patronize before the hell of the German curse came down on us. I was only a small girl then and probably you didn't notice me."

Of course I remembered her decent Jewish family, struggling to survive on the income from their poorly stocked grocery store. I vaguely recalled their scrawny little daughter Sarah, but found it hard to believe she had become this young woman.

As had become customary among us, I asked where she had survived and who else had been with her. She had been in the liquidation transport from Plaszow to Auschwitz with the group of people from our city. My wife Irka, her mother, Mrs. Spiegel, and her sister Kala had also been there, she added. Sarah fell silent and looked away from me, as if to avoid an answering to the expected question.

Finally, she managed to stammer, "They all perished. All of them, including my whole family. All of them were murdered in cold blood by the Germans. I was the only one to survive by a freak accident. I still don't know how to explain it."

For the first time I was learning directly that my wife Irka had not survived. In the few months since the war had ended I had not been able to find out the fate of the women from our town who, in November 1944, had been sent by transport to Auschwitz. There were only disturbing rumors about their fate. Nevertheless, I had continued to hope.

Now I had to know when and how it had happened. Sarah agreed to go with me to the Jewish Information Office where we would be undisturbed.

She told me that when she had learned about today's review of the SS prisoners, she insisted on being included in the group going to Dachau. She hoped to recognize among the murderers not only the Germans, but also those cursed Austrians who had distinguished themselves as the cruelest murderers in our ghetto. Did I remember their names, she asked? She certainly did, and she started to name them.

Nemec from Vienna, Pell, Milas, Nichov, Neumeister, Reiner and especially Lt. Vippert. Did I remember that one? It had been in the fifth action, when single-handed he had manned a machine gun and mowed down about 2,000 victims, Jewish men, women and children, by the mass grave on the outskirts of our city, near the slaughterhouse. She had hoped to recognize them one day, she said with determination. There was a touch of honed steel in her voice.

Sarah began her story, going back to late September or October 1944, when the liquidation transport from Plaszow to Auschwitz had taken place. Somehow the deported had learned that their destination was Auschwitz. The hell of the tightly packed boxcars would be followed by worse.

Upon arrival in Auschwitz, they were subjected to a selection under the direction of the despised Dr. Mengele. After she had passed the inspection and was directed by the monster's white-gloved hand to the group of young and relatively healthy-looking individuals, she witnessed the selection to the very end. The mortal despair of the mothers with their children, and the old and sick being directed into the gas chamber line had remained engraved forever in her memory. She had seen Mrs. Spiegel and my wife Irka and her sister Kala approaching the selection spot. Mengele had directed the mother to the death line, and both her daughters to the slave labor group.

Sarah stopped speaking. Her face muscles convulsed, and she burst into unrestrained sobbing. It was a long while before she calmed down.

Both daughters, she said in a trembling voice, had started to follow their mother, despite her protestation. At that point, the SS men had intervened. They had assaulted the two wailing sisters with rifle butts, and had dragged them to the slave group designated by Mengele.

For weeks, the two sisters were like lifeless automatons, clinging to each other in their misery. They had lost their father only a day before, and now their mother in that Auschwitz death factory. Wordless, they kept staring at the dark smoke that poured from the chimneys of the crematorium ovens.

A few weeks later, Sarah continued, most of the group was put aboard a rail transport. Days later they had arrived in the Stutthof Concentration Camp, which was located close to the Baltic Sea. There, in addition to the other miseries of a death camp, the cold weather had added immeasurably to their suffering.

The winter days and weeks had dragged on in a hopeless monotony of hunger, the cold, hard work, abuse, and despair. Then, one day the distant booms of artillery were heard in the east. At first they were faint, and could be heard only in the stillness of the nights. Soon they had become daily, and were clearly getting closer. Hope started to appear in the sunken eyes of the condemned.

Then one day, the German guards formed a tight cordon around the assembled prisoners on the roll call square. With their rifles at the ready and vehement shouting they started to march the prisoners toward the sea. At the shore, they shouted orders to continue marching onto the ice of the frozen sea. The Germans had formed a line facing their victims. At the next command, they fired indiscriminately into the crowd of the defenseless, screaming prisoners.

Sarah's face was terror-stricken. She lowered her head, and her body began to tremble out of control. I put my arm around her shoulders in an attempt to comfort her. Finally, she was able to resume.

The next thing she could recall was a small room in a peasant hut. It was very quiet and warm. She noticed an old woman slumbering in a corner. Quietly she tried to figure things out. Suddenly, the memory of the carnage on the Baltic Sea ice had come back in all its horror. She sat up screaming violently beyond control.

The old woman woke up and hobbled to her. The woman was very bent with age. Her hair was white, and her face and forehead were crisscrossed with dense wrinkles. A sweet smile of concern was on her face.

She put her arms around Sarah, and started to calm her with words of a strange language mixed with German expressions. Shaking with fear, Sarah had become hysterical and had tried to get out of bed and flee. The creaking of the door startled her, and she heard the deep voice of a man.

He, too, was very old and slightly bent, but he still looked strong. His white hair was falling over his ears, down to this chin. In the windburnt face furrowed with deep wrinkles, his keen, blue eyes had been assessing the situation. He approached Sarah's bed. The woman introduced him as her husband, a good man not to be frightened of, she assured Sarah. The man's calm words had the same soothing quality of the voice of Sarah's grandfather when, during her childhood, he had comforted her after a fall.

The man spoke to Sarah in German, which she understood. He said they were Prussians, not to be mistaken for Germans. He asked her to calm down, and assured her that she was out of any danger. The cursed Germans had gone. The Russians were pursuing them, and closing in on Berlin.

While the old woman urged her to drink hot milk, the man was getting out of his outdoor clothing. Vit and Marik sat at the side of her bed. Their kind faces finally put her at ease.

Vit started to bring her up to date. It had been early in the morning about ten days before. He had gone to the seashore, hoping to find some drift wood for their stove. As he walked along the shore, something bulky in the water had caught his attention. It was a human body so small that he thought it was a child. He had been certain that there was life in that body, and he had carried Sarah to his home.

Fortunately, the couple had experience in treating people who had been rescued from the icy waters of the Baltic Sea. With utmost difficulty, they had succeeded in bringing life back into the chilled body of the young girl, taking turns watching over her day and night.

Sarah had been running a high fever, and had been crying and screaming in a language which they had not understood. They had been sure that this was an inmate of the infamous concentration camp in Stutthof, whom they had rescued from the sea. They would keep it a secret as long as the Germans were around.

Sarah's face reflected love as she told me about the two noble people. She stayed with them for weeks until she had recovered. Then she had travelled to Poland in hope of finding surviving members of her family.

The search had been in vain. Finally, faced with the very hostile attitude of the Polish people to returning Jews, she had joined a group of Jewish survivors who illegally went over the Polish and Czech borders to the American Zone of Germany.

Presently, she lived in the D.P. camp in Feldafing. She hoped to soon be included in a group of former concentration camp inmates who, under the auspices of the *Bricha*, planned to go over the Brenner Pass to Italy, and then to Palestine.

For days, I could not stop thinking about the selection scene in Auschwitz, and the bloody massacre on the frozen Baltic Sea. My wound, which had seemed to form a scab, had been opened again. The pain and nightmares would not leave me for a long time.

After all I had been through, I had not been able to mourn until now. The multitudes of the murdered had become faceless, indistinct legions of victims. It took the account of one witness relating the detail, place, time, and circumstances of the death of persons dear to me, to make my loss and pain personal. Now I could personally mourn.

After a while, Sarah's revelation became the spiritual equivalent of having attended a funeral for my wife Irka, nicknamed in our family "Doncia" (Ukrainian for "little daughter"), for her sister Kala, and for their mother and father. My mourning lasted for many days to come.

I began to wish that my hatred for the Germans would manifest itself in something that would bring relief to my pent-up emotions. Eventually, I came to realize that just as mourning for millions of victims was beyond human capacity, so was hating a faceless multitude of enemies.

SIXTEEN

Gina arrived unexpectedly at the end of the month. She and her mother had settled in the Stuttgart D.P. camp. She joked about the new label under which we have become known since the end of the war. After being liberated as K-Zetlers, concentration camp inmates, we have become D.P.'s. When will we again be just like other people with no labels attached? she asked resentfully.

She told us that the Stuttgart camp occupied two blocks of multi-story buildings in the city. It was not a camp at all, but that was how the authorities designated all the locations where liberated people lived from the Vaihingen Concentration Camp near Stuttgart. Defiantly, they started calling the settlement on the Reinsburg Street the Radomer Center.

With real admiration, Gina described the life of the survivors in the Radomer Center, where the harmonious cooperation of the military administration, UNRRA, and the Joint Distribution Office managed to help the survivors establish a semblance of a dignified existence. The inmates did not have to eat in the cafeteria. They could receive food supplies and prepare meals in their own kitchens. This meant a lot to their self-esteem.

Encouraged by the sensitive and enlightened American UNRRA management, the few hundred inmates enthusiastically started to organize various civic institutions, to meet their health and educational needs. They were publishing their own news bulletin.

For us, this was hard to believe, because the D.P. camps we knew were run by the military occupation authorities and presented a different, sorry picture. The camps were surrounded by barbed wire fences with guards on continuous duty. The inmates had to live in barracks with two- or three-story bunk beds as the only furniture. Meals were served three times a day, and inmates had to wait in long lines to get food servings. They could not cook for themselves.

We were angry that our American friends had so readily accepted the authoritarian German ways of treating those who were supposedly liberated.

One day Gina wanted to visit the Feldafing D.P. camp near Munich. She had learned that some people she had known from Warsaw and Radom lived there, and she was anxious to see them. I volunteered to take her.

We had to register and obtain passes at the guard post of the Jewish militia, which was under the command of the military occupation authorities.

In the Feldafing administration office, we found out that the persons we wanted to see lived in the same barrack. This was of no surprise. The survivors liked to cling together and form groups of people who shared something common in their past. We located six people including a man and his wife. All were from Warsaw, and most were from the printers group. They greeted Gina with the rejoicing of grownups who had found a dear lost youngster. They had heard that she and her mother had survived, but seeing her in person, that was different. They hugged her, laughed, asked questions, and exchanged information about other people.

When I was introduced, the group greeted me warmly. They knew about the work we had been doing at the Jewish Information Office in Dachau, and expressed their appreciation for it.

In the part of the barrack they occupied, they managed to create a semblance of privacy by arranging their two-deck bunks in a group. The couple had blankets draped around their bunks.

Without complaining, they spoke of their great longing to leave German soil and live in a place where they could start a new life. High on the list was Palestine, where they could contribute to building their own country, a Jewish country, separate and independent.

To my surprise, these people hardly resented the fence and the guards around the camp, but rather viewed them as a kind of protection from the German population. On the other hand, they voiced deep resentment over the hostile attitude of some of the American occupational authorities.

Only a few days before, they told us, M.P.'s had raided the camp at night. The M.P.'s surrounded their barrack and rudely woke them up, shouting orders to get to one place in the barrack. They tore all the bedding from the bunks, and searched through the belongings of the terrified inmates. They confiscated anything they pleased.

These raids had taken place often under the guise of combating the black market.

A man named Natan became very agitated during this conversation. He worked as a translator for the Americans in a nearby army unit. Recently he had gotten a $5.00 bill from the captain as thanks for a job well done. At night it was under his pillow with a few other items that he usually carried in his pockets. When he rushed to the indicated place in the barrack, his belongings were left on the bunk. A raider discovered his $5.00 bill and demanded in a loud cursing voice that the so-and-so black marketer step out. Natan did not step out, and nobody betrayed him. When they left, they took the bill and other personal items.

A few days later I accompanied Gina to the railroad station. While boarding the train she remembered that she had gotten in touch with Sofia and Ala as she had promised during her first visit in Dachau. She was certain that by now they had moved to the Radomer Center in Reinsburg Street. The shrill conductor's whistle sounded, and the train left the station before I had a chance to thank her.

When I entered the office, Yosef stopped his work on a

file, and remarked that if I kept on being foolish much longer, somebody smarter would snatch her right from under my nose. I got his point.

We had about finished moving the office from the camp, and secured living quarters in town. I had found a room in the attic of a one-family house very close to the office.

On that last moving day, I transferred my very few personal belongings into a jeep. They consisted mainly of books I had appropriated from the SS library in the camp shortly after the liberation. It was quite a collection of German pseudo-scientific research work pertaining to Jews. The books concentrated on mental and physical characteristics which supposedly were common to all Jews. An unbelievable collection of German-Nazi rubbish colored by hate, it mirrored the gutter intellectual level of that society. Why was I curious to read all that garbage? Perhaps because it proved to me once again that my deadly enemy had a sick mentality.

The jeep had just turned into the Nibelungen Strasse when a woman's voice on the American Army Radio intoned the ancient words of *Kol Nidre*. The singer had a beautiful voice. She was rendering the melody and words with deep feeling.

The time and place where the radio carried the majestic tune of the most revered prayer of the Jewish people created an unreality. I was moved to the innermost part of my soul, marveling at the words imploring the Almighty to forgive any vows which would be hastily made and not fulfilled during the coming year.

Asking forgiveness for such a transgression, after all that had been inflicted on us in recent years, was beyond my comprehension. The wounds were still bleeding, and the victims should be concerned about making a future vow they might not fulfill? It made me wonder and marvel about the makeup of our Jewish heritage.

On the other hand, I thought, there was historical precedent. These same vows had been pronounced hundreds of years ago by the Jewish people when they were facing the Catholic Holy Inquisition in Spain and elsewhere in Europe. The same vows have been pronounced year after year for ages, despite the persecutions and the pogroms inflicted on the Jews by the people they have been living with for many centuries.

Only one year ago I had been a part of a hopeless, desperate congregation when we had pronounced the same vows during that *Kol Nidre* evening in Plaszow. Only one year ago our group of miserable remnants had faced annihilation without hope for survival.

Absolutely incredible, I thought, as the American jeep loaded with my meager possessions pulled up in front of our Jewish Information Office.

The majestic tune of *Kol Nidre* still reverberated in my ears as I opened the door to the office. A feeling of humbleness came over me. I recalled the beginning of this organization. We were a few miserable survivors who could hardly walk after the liberation. Nevertheless we had organized ourselves to represent the interests of Jewish concentration camp survivors from all nationalities. We were stubborn enough to overcome all the obstacles in our way, and we had succeeded.

I could not help feeling gratified at what we had accomplished. Then it occurred to me that we had done what all the countless generations of Jews had done after every disaster they had suffered. Like all of them, we had started to rebuild our lives. Our ancestors must have passed this strength on to us without our knowing it.

Gina, 1989.

POSTSCRIPT

As time passed, the Jewish Information Office took on more and more the character of a civil governing body. It represented the Jews living in the town of Dachau, in their dealings with the Americans and the local German authorities.

At the end of 1945 and even more in 1946, there was a substantial influx of Jews to the American Zone of occupied Germany. They were fleeing from Poland, Czechoslovakia, Hungary, and Rumania where, on their return, the population had met them with violent hostility. Virulent anti-Semitism had been fueled in the non-Jewish population, by the prospect of having to return Jewish properties to their rightful owners.

The culmination of this hostility was reached in July 1946 in the city of Kielce, Poland, where many Jewish survivors were massacred in an ugly pogrom. Cardinal Hlond of the local Catholic diocese refused to intervene or condemn the pogrom. A number of those seeking refuge found their way to Dachau. The J.I.O. gave them major help in locating living quarters and finding their way in the new environment.

In November 1945, the war criminals trial began in Nuremberg, Germany. The spectacle of the top German-Nazi criminals being tried under civilized rules by the victorious Allies gave me no satisfaction. For me, there could be no new revelations, nor could justice be done. I could not think of a punishment great enough to fit their crimes. Nothing could ever expose them to the sufferings of seeing their parents, wives, and children being starved, tortured, gassed and cremated. I assumed that the war criminals were going to be sentenced to death. But death would not be

139

sufficient; and what about those many millions of other Germans who not only approved but actively helped the war criminals execute their policies and laws? All this made me an impassive follower of that trial.

The same month the trials started, I was electrified by the news that my sister Pepa and her five-year-old daughter, Rysia, had survived and were living in Krakow, Poland, under assumed Polish names, in order to hide their Jewish identity. Pepa received my letter just days after an acquaintance had told her that I had perished in Auschwitz.

More excitement! One day in December 1945, Moshe the barber chanced to meet an acquaintance, Yulek Ackerman, in the Deutsches Museum. Ackerman had recently crossed the Polish border to Germany. In a shelter for refugees in Berlin, he had found my youngest sister, Mania. Mania had returned to Germany after trying to find family in Poland, and was very sick with pneumonia. Ackerman took care of her, and after she recovered, helped her come to Munich. Moshe told Yulek about me, and so I became reunited with Mania. She and Yulek were married soon after.

Gina and I continued to see each other either where she lived with her mother, Mrs. Rachela Rachman, in Stuttgart, or in Dachau, whenever she came for a visit. We were very much in love. Amazingly, life now held out the promise of happiness.

On March 9, 1946, with our friend Yozek as a witness, we were married by the *Burgemeister* (the Mayor) of the city of Dachau. Ten days later our traditional Jewish wedding took place in Stuttgart. Gina's mother flooded the apartment with flowers. Cantor Siegelman from Dachau performed the Jewish ceremony, and presented his hand-written Ketubah, the ancient Hebrew marriage agreement, to Gina.

My friend Yozek and my new brother-in-law Yulek signed as witnesses. Our friends from Dachau and Stuttgart celebrated with us late into the night.

That month I also received a communication from my Aunt Gusti, my father's sister, in Brooklyn, N.Y. Her brother, my Uncle Jacob in Tel Aviv, happened to be listening to a radio broadcast from Switzerland in which were announced names of Jewish survivors in the Dachau concentration camp. The announcer said that the lists had been prepared by some survivors who had formed a Jewish Information Office. They heard the name of their nephew, Joel Sack, among the names.

In the letters that followed, Aunt Gusti informed me that she was securing affidavits for us all, including Gina's mother. In July 1946 my sister Pepa and her little daughter illegally crossed dangerous borders and came to me in Dachau.

A few days later I took little Rysia for a walk. At the gate of the Dachau concentration camp, I impulsively sat on the ground and faced the camp. The memory of my arrival at that spot, ending the death march from the Flossenburg concentration camp, flashed before my closed eyes.

The fantasy of being reunited with my little niece, which had come to me in that time of utter misery, now became a wonderful reality. I remember the vow I had made, that if the improbable ever happened, and both the child and I survived, I would bring her to this spot. There we were together.

My niece's voice, asking me about the words, "Arbeit Macht Frei" on the gate, made me open my eyes. This time my anxiety disappeared.

Yozek and my sister Pepa got married in December 1946. Little Rysia was very happy to have a father. After a two-year wait, they got their visas and went to America. Before he left, Yozek transferred the files of the Jewish Information Office to the Central Jewish Committee for Bavaria in Munich.

Gina and I were fortunate. We passed the medical exams at the American Embassy. Finally in April 1947, we embarked on the *S.S. Bremen*, the former troop carrier *Ernie Pyle*, for the voyage to the United States. To our great joy, Gina was pregnant with our first child. America became our new homeland.